WINTER KEPT US WARM

Queer Film Classics

Edited by Matthew Hays and Thomas Waugh

The enduring commercial success of LGBTQ2I films over recent generations offers proof of widespread interest in queer film within both pop culture and academia. Not only are recent works riding the wave of the new maturity of queer film culture, but a century of queer and proto-queer classics are in busy circulation thanks to a burgeoning online queer cinephile culture and have been brought back to life by omnipresent festivals and revivals. Meditations on individual films from queer perspectives are particularly urgent, unlocking new understandings of political as well as aesthetic and personal concerns.

Queer Film Classics at McGill-Queen's University Press emphasizes good writing, rigorous but accessible scholarship, and personal, reflective thinking about the significance of each film – writing that is true to the film, original, and enlightening and enjoyable for film buffs, scholars, and students alike. Books in the series are short – roughly 40,000 words – but well illustrated and allow for considerable depth. Exploring historical, authorial, and production contexts and drawing on filmic analysis, these open-ended essays also develop the author's personal interests or a subjective reading of the work's sexual identity discourses or reception. The series aims to meet the diversity, quality, and originality of classics in the queer film canon, broadly conceived, with equally compelling writing and critical insight. Books in the series have much to teach us, not only about the art of film but about the queer ways in which films can transmit our meanings, our stories, and our dreams.

L'Homme blessé
Robert Payne

Boys Don't Cry
Chase Joynt and Morgan M Page

Orlando
Russell Sheaffer

Appropriate Behavior
Maria San Filippo

Midnight Cowboy
Jon Towlson

À tout prendre et *Il était une fois dans l'Est*
Julie Vaillancourt

Anders als die Andern
Ervin Malakaj

Maurice
David Greven

Winter Kept Us Warm
Chris Dupuis

WINTER KEPT US WARM

Chris Dupuis

McGill-Queen's University Press
Montreal & Kingston | London | Chicago

ISBN 978-0-2280-2032-5 (cloth)
ISBN 978-0-2280-2033-2 (paper)
ISBN 978-0-2280-2034-9 (ePDF)
ISBN 978-0-2280-2035-6 (ePUB)

Legal deposit second quarter 2024
Bibliothèque nationale du Québec

Printed in Canada on acid-free paper that is 100% ancient forest free (100% post-consumer recycled), processed chlorine free

Funded by the Government of Canada | Financé par le gouvernement du Canada | Canada | Canada Council for the Arts | Conseil des arts du Canada

We acknowledge the support of the Canada Council for the Arts.
Nous remercions le Conseil des arts du Canada de son soutien.

McGill-Queen's University Press in Montreal is on land which long served as a site of meeting and exchange amongst Indigenous Peoples, including the Haudenosaunee and Anishinabeg nations. In Kingston it is situated on the territory of the Haudenosaunee and Anishinaabek. We acknowledge and thank the diverse Indigenous Peoples whose footsteps have marked these territories on which peoples of the world now gather.

Library and Archives Canada Cataloguing in Publication

Title: Winter kept us warm / Chris Dupuis.
Names: Dupuis, Chris, author.
Description: Series statement: Queer film classics | Includes bibliographical references and index.
Identifiers: Canadiana (print) 20230509649 | Canadiana (print) 20230509673 | Canadiana (ebook) 20230509673 | ISBN 9780228020325 (hardcover) | ISBN 9780228020332 (softcover) | ISBN 9780228020349 (PDF) | ISBN 9780228020356 (EPUB)
Subjects: LCSH: Winter kept us warm (Motion picture) | LCSH: Secter, David—Criticism and interpretation. | LCSH: Homosexuality in motion pictures.
Classification: LCC PN1997.W56 D87 2024 | DDC 791.43/72—dc23

For Patricia Wilson
For everything
Forever

Contents

Figure F1
Dave and Jack in 1927's *Wings*, winner of the world's first best picture Oscar, engaging in what is arguably the world's first gay male movie kiss: "You – you know there is nothing in the world that means so much to me as your friendship …"

Foreword

The Heart of Light, the Silence

In Chris Dupuis's wonderfully wry social history of *Winter Kept Us Warm*, readers are invited to consider this film within a troubled continuum of queer cinematic "friendship." From the deliciously overwrought death kiss of *Wings*, to the shattering beach hand job of *Moonlight*, Chris positions *Winter*'s convoluted bromance as a stubborn, nervous, understated outlier, shivering amongst its more flamboyant mid-sixties cine peers, framing the film within the National Film Board's "small story" vérité tradition, and convincingly arguing that the film refuses the two dominant queer tendencies of the day: on the one hand, the gloriously high-stakes neo-realist melodramatic excess of *The Leather Boys* or *Accattone*, and on the other, the experimental underground radicalism of a Warhol or an Anger. The book explores how the film's near erasure from our cinematic memory is a complex product of warring social, critical, and cultural forces over these ensuing six decades: the rise (and fall) of subsequent generations of queer cinemas, in all their labyrinthine glories, the parallel inventions, transformations, and convolutions of both our English Canadian film industry, and equally, our parallel Canadian indie tradition, and perhaps most of all, the aching question of what we viewers think we really want from our closeted "friendship" stories, past and present.

In this nuanced appreciation of *Winter*, Chris has persuasively restored the film to its rightful place (warts and all) within a queer indie Toronto canon (which is already well represented in this growing Queer Classics series, and includes monographs on Lynne Fernie and Aerlyn Weissman's *Forbidden Love*, Patricia Rozema's *I've Heard the Mermaids Singing*, Deepa Mehta's *Fire*, and my own *Zero Patience*) celebrating this work of tender chutzpah that indisputably gave inspiration to so many of us who came up through the seventies and eighties. Podeswa and Rozema, Fung and La Bruce, Fernie and Hoolboom, Mohabeer and myself, among others: *Winter* gave us the courage to likewise rub our pennies together, stick our necks out, and dare against the odds to make *our* first queer features.

Throughout, the text invaluably insists on the material conditions that shaped David Secter's unique production: the $8,000 budget (because no one was willing to take a chance on a bunch of student first-timers), the necessary closetry of the process (with much of the cast and crew never realizing they were actually making a gay film), the improvisatory hubris of a script unfolding on a wing and a prayer. Watching the film again through the author's eyes, I was dumbfounded by the logistics that David was able to pull off, against the odds: no-permit guerilla shoots outside an actual Harry Belafonte concert at the O'Keefe Centre, his team waiting weeks for the perfect blizzard, six cameras standing by to catch sunrise on the quad, the wrangling of over a hundred background performers for the dining room scenes. (His Hart House shower scene brought back fond memories of my own adventures, likewise shooting naked butts and tits in the same locker room two decades later for my video hybrid, *Moscow Does Not Believe in Queers*.)

Perhaps most crucially, Chris reminds us that *Winter* is above all a student film – a student film about students – indeed, a student *feature* film about students that was made when there were quite literally no film schools in Canada, and barely any features of any kind being made in English Canada. As I rewatch Secter's ambitious staging of scenes on diverse University of Toronto locations, I think about how newer student features, including queer features, have sometimes been supported in the last decade with visionary resources of cash and mentorship. Looking at Secter's hallway scenes, I'm reminded of Matt Johnson's 2016 moon-landing epic *Operation Avalanche*,

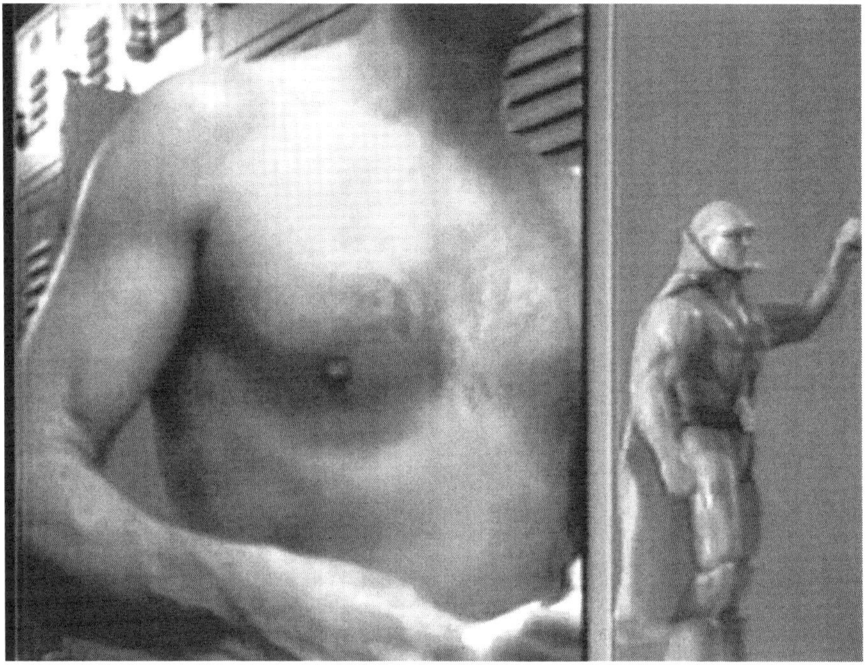

Figure F2
Hart House lockers and tits, *Moscow Does Not Believe in Queers*, 1986.

where he used the corridors of our film department at York to stand in for the CIA's Langley complex, circa 1967. Watching Secter's theatre scenes, I'm reminded of Chase Joynt's brilliant transgender talk-show scenes, in his 2022 hybrid docudrama *Framing Agnes.* Both are award-winning features, celebrated at international film fests, with the former funded by Lionsgate, while the latter was co-produced with York through Telefilm Canada's *Talent to Watch* program. That both were able to raise substantial budgets, and still be made as "student films," amply illustrates the extraordinary sea change that

Figure F3
Winter Kept Us Warm, 1965.

has been accomplished in the material cultures of both film education and film production during this past half-century.

I've not met David yet and so haven't had the opportunity to thank him personally for the audacity and tenacity of *Winter*'s "small story," a film which continues to warm us all with its indelible depiction of a tender friendship that fails. With this volume, Chris plugs in the dorm room kettle and asks us all to join him in a cup of contemplative cinematic tea, appreciating the remarkable singularity of *Winter*. Speaking back against what sometimes seems like a current *wasteland* of queer Canadian features, and thinking more on

David and Chris's unique contributions, and most of all, inspired by *Winter*'s final quiet scene, trembling with electric longing, I offer some words of T.S. Eliot back to both of them, with thanks (just thirty-six lines below the source of David's title): "Looking into the heart of light, the silence."

JOHN GREYSON

Acknowledgments

Thanks to the Queer Film Classics team Jonathan Crago, Matthew Hays, and Thomas Waugh. To Stéphanie Verge for supreme editing assistance. ("Thank God I'm not the only freak here!") To Lauren Allen for interview transcription. To Marcin Wisniewski and Ash Kinney d'Harcourt for research assistance. To Martín Zícari for being there. To the interviewees Bruce Bell, James Dubro, Janet Amos, Andrew Kushner, Joel Secter, Joe Medjuck, Joy Fielding, Paul Hoffert, Robert Fothergill, and Ron B. Thomson. And to David Secter, for this film and the many hours of conversation that made this book possible. This project was produced with the support of the Toronto Arts Council, the Ontario Arts Council, and the Canada Council for the Arts.

Synopsis

Made with a budget of $8,000 by David Secter, a twenty-two-year-old English major with no filmmaking experience, *Winter Kept Us Warm* is widely considered English Canada's first queer film. Released in 1965, *Winter* tells the story of two college students, Doug (John Labow), a popular senior, and Peter (Henry Tarvainen), a shy freshman, who form an unlikely bond over two semesters at the University of Toronto.

The film opens as Peter arrives from the tiny northern Ontario town of Capreol and Doug returns from a summer working at a Hamilton steel mill. Peter initially struggles to make friends, spending the bulk of his time alone in his room. The pair first meet during a hazing ritual in the dining hall, where Doug humiliates Peter in front of a group of fellow students. Later that evening they cross paths again in the library, where Peter is borrowing a copy of T.S. Eliot's *The Waste Land*. Embarrassed by his earlier behaviour, Doug apologizes, though Peter remains shaken and suspicious. Over the course of the fall, a camaraderie grows as Doug, still remorseful, takes Peter under his wing. Doug's protective instincts gradually evolve into a latent romantic interest, crystallized by a playful outdoor romp in December, after the first snowfall of the year.

After the Christmas break, the relationship suddenly becomes complicated when Peter starts dating Sandra (Janet Amos), an older student with whom he's performing in a campus production of Henrik Ibsen's *Ghosts*. Doug's attraction is further ignited during some locker room horseplay following the college winter carnival. Doug becomes jealous of Sandra as Peter pulls away from him, asserting his own identity. At the same time, Doug's long-time girlfriend Bev (Joy Fielding, credited as Joy Tepperman) has grown suspicious, noting that Doug has been losing interest in her since Peter arrived on campus, and hinting the boys might be romantically involved. The film builds to a climax where Doug assaults Peter after learning he has had sex with Sandra. Left alone, Doug is forced to confront his feelings. He returns to the library, where he begins reading *The Waste Land*, and the realization of his romantic interest suddenly comes into focus.

Credits

Winter Kept Us Warm © 1965, released 27 September 1965 (Commonwealth Film Festival), Canada, English, 81 minutes
Distributed by CFMDC, Canadian International Pictures, and the Film-maker's Cooperative
Produced by Varsity Productions

Director
David Secter

Executive Producer
Ron B. Thomson

Producer
David Secter

Scenario
David Secter

Dialogue
Ian Porter, John Clute, and the cast

Music
Paul Hoffert

Cinematography
Robert Fresco and Ernest Meershoek

Film Editor
Michael Foytényi
Associate Editor
George Appleby

Budget
$8,000

Principal Cast

John Labow	Doug
Henry Tarvainen	Peter
Joy Fielding (Tepperman)	Bev
Janet Amos	Sandra
Iain Ewing	Artie
Jack Messinger	Nick
Larry Greenspan	Larry
Sol Mandlsohn	Hall Porter

WINTER KEPT US WARM

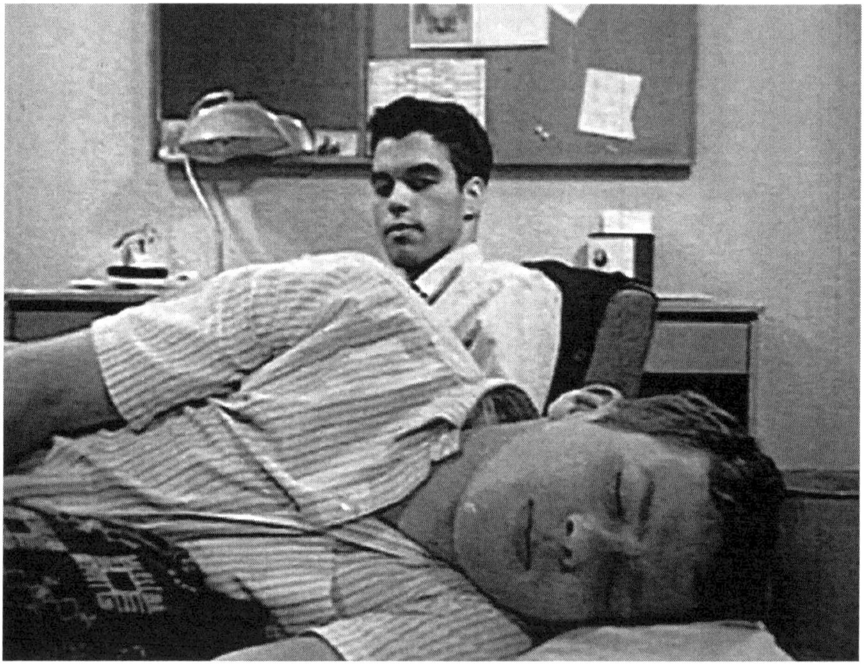

Figure 1
Doug (John Labow) looks longingly at Peter (Henry Tarvainen).

Chapter 1

A Footnote in History

In the final scene of *The Best of Secter & the Rest of Secter* (Joel Secter's 2005 documentary about his uncle), David Secter sits on a beach, the setting sun bathing the mountains behind him in orange and pink. "I certainly haven't made it as far as the industry is concerned," he says. "And unless things change in the next few years, I assume I'll go down at the most as a little asterisk, a footnote in history."

In 1965, Secter's debut feature *Winter Kept Us Warm* emerged as an unlikely success story of the nascent Anglo-Canadian film scene. A fourth-year student at the University of Toronto, Secter had relocated from Winnipeg three years earlier. The city's flourishing gay scene meant sex was easy to find. But he yearned for a deeper connection, ultimately developing a strong though unreciprocated interest in his straight roommate. After a failed plan to travel the world making a documentary the summer between third and fourth year, he decided to pursue filmmaking on his own. The subject of his big screen debut would be his failed romance. As an English major with no formal training or industry contacts, his jump to cinema was, to the casual observer, an act of naive audacity. Fortunately, his inexperience meant he had no idea of the challenges that lay before him. Backed by a volunteer crew and a team of amateur actors, Secter borrowed some equipment and set out to tell his story. The result was a work blending autobiography and imagination, offering a portrait of queer attraction in the stiflingly homophobic environment of a mid-twentieth-century Canadian university.

Secter's decision to enter the movie business came at an inopportune moment. In the early 1960s, the advent of television had pushed Anglo-Canadian film production into decline. With limited domestic financing and little interest from international producers, getting a project off the ground was a monumental task. Technically proficient crew were in short supply, in part because the country didn't yet have a film school, and ambitious actors often flocked to Los Angeles, leaving a limited pool of local talent. Beyond the constraints of the industry, producing a queer film was itself remarkable. In a decade when homosexuality was still illegal and gay bashing a common college extracurricular, the project was both a creative and personal risk. Against all odds, Secter's inaugural effort blew up: it was selected to open the Commonwealth Film Festival and became the first Anglo-Canadian fiction feature to screen at Cannes. Lauded by critics at home and abroad, *Winter* played art-house theatres in Europe and college campuses across the US and Canada. With his combination of wide-eyed optimism and youthful naivety, Secter had pulled off a nearly unimaginable coup, for himself and for Canadian cinema. This, unfortunately, would be the high point of his career.

I first saw *Winter* at some point in the early 2000s when a Toronto indie paper announced a rare screening, hailing it an unmissable queer classic. At the time, I was trying to expand my knowledge of queer cultural history, and this seemed like an opportunity to learn. At best, I was hoping for a life-changing experience. In the end, all I saw was a glitchy black-and-white film with choppy editing and stilted dialogue. I left disappointed and *Winter* quickly faded from my mind. Some years later, I saw the film again and my experience was radically different. An archaically dull picture that had barely sustained my attention was now a heart-wrenching portrait of longing, confusion, and unrequited love. Ironically, not long before my first viewing, I'd lived out a nearly identical situation with a guy in my own university dorm. Like Secter, I'd poured my heart into a script, which I then staged as a play for my undergraduate thesis. Yet, despite our parallel experiences, I wasn't able to see what Secter was trying to show me.

Part of the reason, I think, had to do with coming out in the late-1990s in the wake of the AIDS crisis. Queer politics were radical. Rage was palpable. Posters and buttons screamed "Identify Yourself!" and "Silence = Death." My suburban childhood had little connection to queer life besides Madonna and *Fashion Television*. But when I moved into the city for university, queerness was kicking down the door and screaming in your face. The fact that it was so easy to spot also shaped my understanding of how to look for it. As I was piecing together my identity, the historical references that resonated were usually the ones steeped in that revolutionary spirit. So when I encountered more subtle examples of queerness, I often missed them – that first viewing of *Winter* being a perfect example.

My initial take on the film is broadly illustrative of a larger pattern experienced by contemporary audiences. As I was starting the research process for this book, I informally polled a number of twenty-something queer folks for their thoughts on the work. None of them had even heard of it. When I had a few of them watch the film, they shrugged it off, much as I had initially done. Despite its broader historical significance, to them it didn't feel relevant. The fact that these younger folks were unfamiliar with Secter's work shouldn't have been a surprise; beyond a scant Wikipedia entry and similarly sparse IMDB page, *Winter* had almost no online presence. And despite the relative importance attached to the film by a handful of critics, it was barely mentioned in the "Best Queer Movies" lists populating various websites. How does a film so radical in its approach, so lauded upon its release, and so important to the history of queer and Canadian cinema, virtually disappear from the broader canon, rendering its director, in his own words, "a footnote"?

It's possible, of course, that *Winter*'s absence from the broader cultural consciousness was just an oversight, perhaps an unsurprising one. Queer film exploded in the decades following its release, first with the post-Stonewall freedom of the early 1970s and again with the AIDS crisis in the 1980s. Maybe

Secter's shy love story was simply eclipsed by the radical work that came in its wake? While this may account for its disappearance from film history, it remains an odd thing for queer Canadians to forget.

As a historical object, part of *Winter*'s value is in how clearly it encapsulates the realities of gay life in the context in which it was made. It's an expression of queer sexuality produced in a time and place where that sexuality was criminalized, a fact reflected in both the delicate storytelling and the remarkably cautious nature of the production. It reveals how queer stories could be told in this time and place – a romantic interest that's never articulated because neither the characters nor the audience would have been able to deal with it.

When I started this book, I thought the process would be fairly straightforward: assemble available writing on the film and complement it with some interviews. Instead, I ended up taking a deep dive into gay life in early-1960s Toronto (something I knew little about) and the history of Canadian film production during that same period (a subject I understood even less). Chapter 2 addresses this contextual framework. Chapter 3 covers Secter's path to filmmaking and the production of the work. Chapter 4 reflects on contemporaneous and current analyses of the film. Chapter 5 asks what might be learned from this story. As there was comparatively little written on the film, I thought my goal would be to make a definitive statement about Secter's work, its place in cinema history, and its contemporary relevance. What I've come to realize is that I'm simply tapping into a conversation about this film, and about queer history more broadly, that's already been happening for a long time. My job is to figure out where I fit into it and how I can help it continue.

Chapter 2

When *Winter* Was Made

The 1960s have always been a mythical time in my imagination. As a child, my understanding of the decade was shaped largely by my parents, who experienced it as children themselves. Family photos show well-groomed men in pressed slacks and demurely dressed ladies in tasteful hats – snapshots of a time when authority was respected and a quiet optimism hung in the air. These pictures are, of course, only part of the story. For the first half of the 1960s, images like these were the dominant cultural iconography; the mud-pits of Woodstock, the horrors of Vietnam, and the terrifying face of Charles Manson only arrived as the decade drew to a close. This stark contrast leads to perhaps the most cliché thing that can be said about this time: it was a period of change. Along with the struggle for civil rights, the rise of the political left, and the birth of student protests, we saw the dawn of the modern gay rights movement. But during the first half of the decade – the time period this book examines – none of these seismic shifts were assured or even anticipated.

As someone who came out in the 1990s, it can be difficult for me to connect with the realities of gay life in Canada thirty years earlier. Like previous generations, most of my contemporaries spent high school in the closet. Cut off from elders who could support us and without school systems that would protect us, we kept our sexualities secret. The key difference between our cohort and those growing up in the 1960s was the shift to university. In the 1990s,

Figure 2
Secter gets his shot. *The Independent Weekly*, date unknown.

the left-wing slant of student culture at most post-secondary institutions combined with their being located in bigger cities meant coming out was not only possible but encouraged. The college dorm – with its rainbow flags, freely available condoms, and floor upon floor of bedrooms – offered both political and practical space to explore our sexualities. For previous generations, the situation was radically different. Sex-segregated university residences and varsity sports created opportunities for homoerotic tensions (and therefore homophobia) to flourish. Coming out, if it did happen, usually occurred after graduation. The same spaces that offered us the freedom to be who we were kept our ancestors in the closet.

The 1960s saw a gradual transition in Canadian attitudes towards homosexuality, culminating with Bill C-150, the Criminal Law Amendment Act of

1969. The bill decriminalized gay sex in private for men over the age of twenty-one, asserting, as Prime Minister Pierre Elliot Trudeau had famously quipped, that there was no place for the state in the bedrooms of the nation.[1] The change in our legal status and the eventual shift in public perceptions that it precipitated arguably made coming out safer. As was the case with much of what happened in Canadian society at the time, the roots of this shift came from abroad. Homosexual acts had been criminalized throughout the British Empire since the mid sixteenth century. However, it was only in the late nineteenth century that the idea of the homosexual as an *identity* appeared. Homosexuality was no longer something you *did*, it was something you *were*. With this new conception of the homosexual as an individual, a broader conversation began to emerge. Should this behaviour still be criminalized? Or should it be treated through medicine (Foucault 1978, 43)? This debate continued through the 1950s, thanks in large part to the work of American biologist Alfred Kinsey and the Wolfenden Report, a 1957 study commissioned by the British parliament that recommended decriminalization. That's when a radical new idea started to surface: perhaps homosexuals could simply be left alone to go about their lives. Although there was little mention of gay realities at home (the sparse coverage usually touched on murder cases in which a younger man claimed self-defense against an older one threatening his virtue), Canadian media dutifully reported the discussions being had abroad. Characteristically staid, Canadians in the 1950s largely saw homosexuality as something that happened elsewhere.

By the 1960s though, these international dialogues had translated to an uptick in Canadian media coverage. In November 1964, *Other Voices*, an hour-long current affairs show, did a special edition on homosexuality, hosting a discussion of legal, medical, and religious attitudes on the subject, though without any queer people present. In 1967, the Canadian drama series *Wojeck* ran an episode titled "After All, Who's Art Morrison?" about a middle-aged gay man trapped in a blackmail plot. Print media (particularly in Toronto and Montreal) featured articles and letters to the editor debating the topic.

As was the case elsewhere, the Canadian medical community argued about the causes of homosexuality and possible cures, though they largely supported decriminalization.

Surprisingly, some of the most prominent voices in support of gay rights came from the church. Reverend William Barry, a minister at the United Church of Canada went so far as to express support for gay marriage in 1963, saying homosexuality was an inborn quality akin to being left-handed (*Toronto Star* 1963). The Catholic Church also supported decriminalization, insisting that while gay sex was a sin, it shouldn't be seen as a crime (*Toronto Star* 1964). There was no clear consensus on the moral implications of being gay or how the government should deal with the issue, but the fact the conversation was happening at all was critically important for visibility.

Two touchstones in this discourse were a pair of articles penned by Sidney Katz for *Maclean's* magazine in early 1964. "The Homosexual Next Door" and "The Harsh Facts of Life in the Gay World" emphasized both the immutable quality of homosexuality and the sheer size of the community. The articles also mentioned America's first queer publication *One* (a San Francisco magazine about gay life) and the Mattachine Society (an early gay rights organization), critical information for folks looking to connect with a broader international community. Above all, the magazine pieces offered something most Canadians had never heard: the perspective of a gay man. Katz interviewed a subject named Verne Baldwin (later revealed to be trailblazing activist James Egan) about life in the gay world, his struggles with his sexuality, and his experience of falling in love with his best friend at age eighteen – a story that mirrors the one Secter tells in *Winter*.

Katz's writing proved crucial not only in helping the public better understand the realities of gay life and the impacts of discrimination, but in providing information to gays themselves about what awaited them if they came out. The lasting impact of Katz's articles was reiterated by Hugh Brewster in *The Walrus* in 2014. Brewster had come across Katz's work fifty years earlier during his studies at Upper Canada College, a famously conservative all-boys boarding school in midtown Toronto. Learning of a world where men kissed, danced, and dated was eye-opening for a closeted teenager raised by Evangelical Christians. What's more, for Brewster, that world was only six subway stops away – a significantly shorter trip than the ninety-minute bus ride I endured getting downtown from my parents' place.

At the same time media coverage was shifting, Toronto's gay scene was blossoming. By 1964, there were nine gay bars, mostly concentrated in the Yonge and Wellesley area. Typically operating as private members' clubs, no addresses were published and you had to be on a list to get in (McLeod 1996, 281–2). There were also a number of older hotspots, primarily hotel bars which, while not officially gay, tolerated queer clientele largely because they drank steadily, tipped generously, and seldom smashed the furniture (Katz 1964b).[2]

Researching these sites can be difficult, as they were often highly secretive and usually short-lived. This also makes understanding gay culture from this period a challenge, since much of it lived within these spaces. Being queer was like a reverse coat check: heading back to your closeted life at the end of the night, you peeled off your identity and left it at the door. In contrast to contemporary life, where nearly every moment is fanatically documented, records of queer spaces from the early 1960s exist largely in people's memories. Photographs were rare since they could serve as blackmail material or evidence in criminal trials (Churchill 2004, 846). The images we have are mostly restricted to exterior shots, captured not as a means of recording queer life but by architects and archivists documenting the city's diverse building facades.

Conventional media offered a limited window into these spaces and usually adopted a sensationalist tone, particularly in the case of tabloids like *Hush* and *Flash* (Churchill 2004, 827–8). Interestingly, these publications served double duty. They presented homosexuality as an object of disgust to the straight world, while simultaneously providing queer readers with clandestine hints on the city's gay life via op-eds published under pseudonyms like Mother Goose, Lady Bessborough, and Duke Gaylord (Churchill 2004, 827–8). In addition to the information he provided to Katz for the articles in *Maclean's*,

James Egan persuaded two tabloids (*True News Times* and *Justice Weekly*) to print pro-gay articles he'd written in the 1950s and succeeded in getting the *Toronto Telegram* (another famously anti-gay scandal sheet) as well as the *Toronto Star* and the *Globe and Mail* to print his letters calling for decriminalization in the early 1960s (Brewster 2014). While Egan's writings were almost certainly seen by the publishers as a way to fuel outrage (and thereby drive sales), they also served to increase visibility and promote acceptance.

In reaction to a largely conservative mainstream media and the sensationalist weeklies, the decade also saw the birth of Canada's gay press, including Vancouver's ASK *Newsletter* (1964–68), the Toronto publications *Gay* (1964–65) and TWO (1964–66), and several beefcake magazines including *The Male Nude* (1964–68), *Young Flesh* (1964), and Montreal's *Face & Physique* (1962–64; for all the foregoing, see McLeod 1996, 258–76). These publications discussed gay life from a gay perspective. Named for a 1954 supplement published by *One* called "Truth Will Out," TWO provides the most detailed picture of this period. Issues featured physique pictorials, erotic stories, guides for dealing with arrest, and cautious hints about cruising spots. They often skewered homophobic articles from other publications, reprinting and deconstructing certain sections. The magazine also revealed some early cracks in the gay community. Certain writers condemned flamboyant gays, claiming they adversely shaped public perception through stereotypes, and drew unwanted attention to clubs and cruising sites, endangering the whole community – a conflict that persists today.

Alongside queer magazines, writers (particularly Americans) were instrumental in shaping public discourse in Canada. Several novels penned during this period featured queer characters, including Gillian Freeman's *The Leather Boys* (1961) and Christopher Isherwood's *A Single Man* (1964; adapted for the screen in 1964 and 2009 respectively). In 1965, the same year *Winter* was released, Edward A. Lacey published *The Forms of Loss*, Canada's first book of openly gay poetry. Notably, queer characters had already been appearing in dramatic works for some time, including Lillian Hellman's *The Children's*

Figure 3
Boys in the trees: *two Magazine*, May-June 1966.

Hour (1934), Robert Anderson's *Tea and Sympathy* (1953), and several of Tennessee Williams's plays, including *A Streetcar Named Desire* (1947) and *Cat on a Hot Tin Roof* (1955). The characters showcased in these works were always conflicted and often suicidal. While neither validating nor celebratory, these portrayals represented a critical shift by portraying queer characters as actual people rather than monsters or criminals, and offering their stories as subjects for serious reflection instead of perverse fascination.

Film lagged behind other art forms in queer representation, in part because most countries had a specific regulatory body tasked with censoring it. In contrast to the way queer people appeared openly in print and on stage, filmic

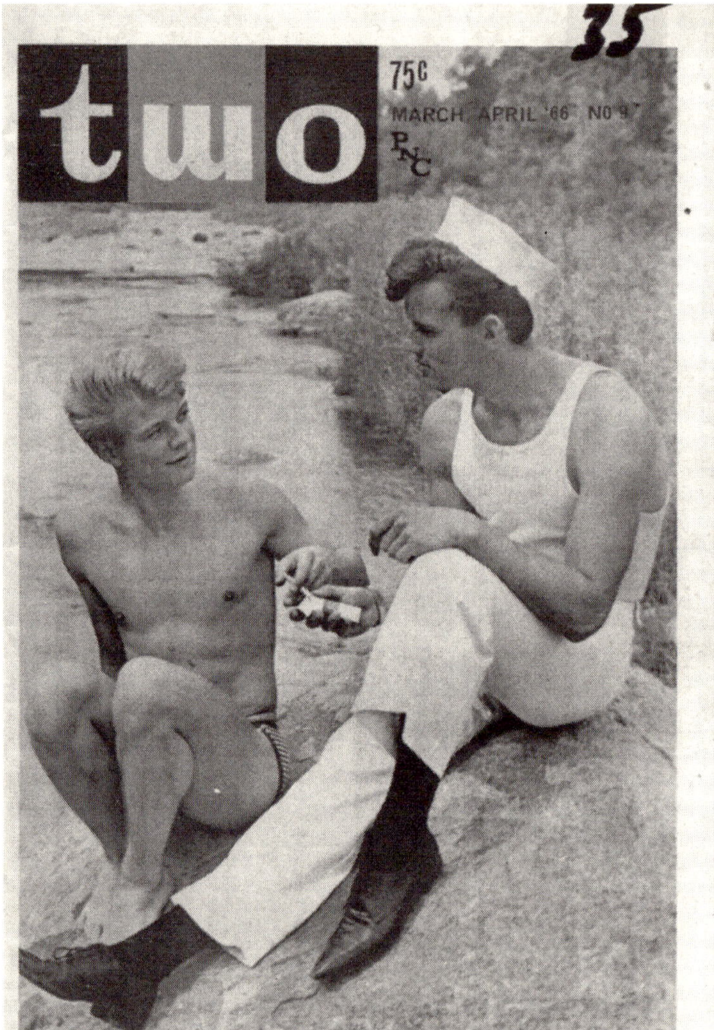

Figure 4
Hello Sailor! *TWO Magazine* March-April 1966.

Figure 5
Face to Face: Scorpio (Bruce Byron) and queer icon James Dean in Kenneth Anger's *Scorpio Rising*.

representations tended to be much more discrete. (The screen adaptations of Anderson's and Williams's works saw references to homosexuality toned down.) Toronto film programmers tried to introduce local audiences to the fledgling US queer cinema scene by showing the works of Kenneth Anger and Jack Smith, but the prints were nearly always seized at the border; screenings, when they did happen, were often met with police presence. (The Bohemian Embassy, a local coffee house that hosted live performance and film, played Anger's *Scorpio Rising* in 1965 after it had been cleared of obscenity, though they declined to show Smith's art house erotica sensation *Flaming Creatures*, fearing the venue would be raided [Cagle 2019, 100].)

During this period, the University of Toronto was very much a microcosm of the wider city. Although the school didn't have a gay rights organization until the end of the decade, the campus was rife with homosexual activity. Hart House, the all-male athletics facility, was referred to by some as "Homo House" for its popularity as a cruising site (Brice 1966). Philosopher's Walk, a leafy passage winding through the sprawling grounds, was also a popular hookup spot (Kinsman 1987, 100). Unlike my university experience in the late 1990s, there were no pink triangle stickers or anti-homophobia posters. Being queer at university was just as dangerous as it was elsewhere; a 1964 article by Heather Dean in the student paper *The Gargoyle* (which was later republished in *TWO*), called gay bashing the school's unofficial varsity sport. The second half of the decade saw increased discussions around homosexuality in the student press and the founding in 1969 of the Homophile Association of U of T (McLeod 1966, 46). For most of the 1960s, though, the university wasn't somewhere that people could safely be out. It also wasn't a place to make a queer film. But David Secter did it anyway.

The implausibility of Secter's foray into queer filmmaking was perhaps rivaled only by his decision to make an independent film at all. At this point, film production was controlled almost entirely by the National Film Board of Canada. Founded in 1939, the state-sponsored studio aimed to combat the dominance of American films by creating uniquely Canadian works for the screen. By 1945, the NFB employed nearly eight hundred people, making it one of the largest film studios in the world (Melnyk 2004, 62). In 1956, the organization relocated from Ottawa to Montreal, strengthening its connection to Francophone filmmakers, who gradually took on a more prominent role within the organization (Melnyk 2004, 73). In the wake of this move, a group of Québécois directors began to develop a new form of documentary. Using an observational improvised shooting style and a participatory approach to its subjects, it was known as cinéma-vérité (direct cinema) and was part of a larger body of work that emerged in Quebec, the US, and France around the same time. (As film theorist Gillian Helfield notes, this new cinema was born of a search for truth "in reaction to the lies and obfuscations promulgated by authoritarian regimes throughout World War II, as well as against the 'classical' documentary conventions by means of which the political ideologies and doctrines of those regimes had been powerfully propagated" [Helfield 2009, 320].) Despite the substantial body of films being made, including a number of Oscar-nominated works, production at the NFB was limited primarily to documentaries and animation. While Quebec had a tradition of narrative film rooted in the burgeoning separatist movement, in English Canada the form was almost non-existent.

With the early 1960s, an alternative to the NFB began to emerge. This new crop of artists worked largely without formal training or access to professional grade equipment. Spiritually and aesthetically, they probably had more in common with their transatlantic counterparts than their fellow countrymen. Inaugurating what film critic Geoff Pevere calls "a campus movie-making movement," this new genre of filmmaking was driven almost entirely by students (Pevere 2003). In 1962, while studying at the Université de Montréal, Denys Arcand, Denis Héroux, and Stéphane Venne made *Seul ou avec d'autres*, a mock documentary gently poking fun at the works of the NFB. (Both Arcand and Venne would later work for the NFB, Arcand as a director and Venne as a composer.) *Seul ou avec d'autres* appeared at Cannes in 1963 as part of *Semaine de la Critique*, a program dedicated to the works of fledgling filmmakers, along with Pierre Perrault and Michel Brault's NFB-produced cinéma-vérité work *Pour la suite du monde*, which featured in the main competition. A year later, Vancouver's Larry Kent released his controversial work *The Bitter Ash*. The film's shocking content (including nudity and frank discussions of sex) kept it out of mainstream cinemas, so Kent screened it on the university film circuit (Pevere 2003). Founded in 1966 and helmed by experimental filmmaker John Hofsess, the McMaster Film Board at Hamilton's McMaster University produced a number of controversial works, which often saw them run afoul of the administration (Broomer 2016a, 3). Most of the MFB films and filmmakers have disappeared, with a few exceptions like future Hollywood A-list director and producer Ivan Reitman. (Hofsess, for his part, came out as gay in the late 1970s, later becoming a prominent voice in queer Canadian

Figure 6
Banned from cinemas: Larry Kent's *The Bitter Ash* was a hit on the college film society circuit.

media [Broomer 2016b].) University of Toronto student David Cronenberg began his first forays into filmmaking with two shorts, *Transfer* (1966) and *From the Drain* (1967), leading to a pair of eerie features *Stereo* (1969) and *Crimes of the Future* (1970). Not wanting to be left out, the University of Manitoba Students' Union made *And No Birds Sing* (1969), a surprisingly well-shot forty-minute look at collegiate life. Perhaps these campus filmmakers, like the artists of cinéma-vérité, were searching for a kind of "truth" in how young people's lives were depicted that they weren't seeing on screen.

Within this milieu, *Winter* is the only film to address queer identity. And in the broader field of Canadian cinema, it's one of just a handful of queer works produced in the 1960s, including Claude Jutra's *À tout prendre* (1963),[3] Mark Rydell's *The Fox* (1967), and Jean-Claude Lord's *Délivrez-nous du mal* (made in 1965 but not released until 1969). As critic Thomas Waugh notes, the founding in 1967 of the Canadian Film Development Corporation (a crown corporation supporting independent production, now known as Telefilm Canada) and Bill C-150 were pivotal moments for Canadian culture, together symbolizing "the official transition from an artisanal cinema to an industrial one (and from sober black and white to glitzy colour), and from underground sexual subcultures to decriminalized sexual constituencies" (Waugh 2001, 104). But the period this book explores takes place before these two watershed moments when the seeds of change were being planted with no guarantee they would take root. In this way, *Winter* serves as a time capsule for an era that might otherwise be forgotten. As someone whose queer life began more than three decades after the film was released, it offers an image of this period that my parents' photo albums and straight culture in general could never give me.

Chapter 3

How *Winter* Was Made

Secter's Path to Filmmaking

David Secter was born 24 March 1943, in the town of Brandon, Manitoba, which had a population of just under 20,000 at the time. The second of three boys, he came from a moderately conservative Jewish family. His mother was a homemaker and his father owned Ricki's, a chain of successful ladieswear stores. In 1950, they moved east to Winnipeg; four years later, Secter began taking drama classes with legendary director and long-time family friend John Hirsch, who co-founded Manitoba Theatre Centre with Tom Hendry. Secter went to Kelvin High School, the same academy Neil Young and Marshall McLuhan attended. He was also active in his local chapter of Aleph Zadik Aleph, an international Jewish fraternal organization.

In the fall of 1960, at age sixteen, he enrolled at the University of Manitoba's General Arts program. By Secter's account, he was a good student and committed to his studies. Friends from high school made up the bulk of his cohort, although he did expand his social circle through the university film society, one of a number of such groups popping up on campuses across the continent. Until then, movies had largely been passive entertainment for Secter; his parents had used the cinema as unofficial post-synagogue daycare, dropping the boys off at a matinee series to keep them occupied and out of trouble for the afternoon. Through the club, Secter saw works by Ingmar Bergman and Federico Fellini, and joined lively post-screening discussions. (No Canadian films were featured in the program, so Secter's initial film culture was grounded in the works of foreign artists.) The club shaped his understanding of film as a medium capable of more than momentary distraction. But he still had no inclination to become a filmmaker since, as he says, "no one was making movies in Canada" (David Secter, interview with author, 17 December 2019).

Despite the university's dynamic social scene, there was no discernible queer life on campus or in the wider city. Winnipeg's tiny gay community was nearly impossible to find and there were no official gay bars until the 1970s. The discreet drinking establishments and cruising spots that did exist, including the beer parlour of the Marlborough Hotel, the Starland Theatre, and "The Hill," an area behind the Manitoba Legislative Building (Stinnett 2019), were accessible only to those in the know and by Secter's own admission, he wasn't sufficiently in the loop. Still a virgin (save for one brief dalliance with a woman), he wasn't certain of what he was looking for sexually. But he was confident he wouldn't find it in his hometown.

Two years into his studies, he decided it was time for a change. Trying to grow as a person while still living at home and surrounded by people he'd known his whole life left him feeling stifled. He transferred to the English language and literature program at the University of Toronto, officially enrolling as a second year student though he already had two years of study under his belt. On 15 September 1962 at 10:00 a.m., he boarded a train that would take him on the twenty-nine-hour journey to his new home. Arriving at Union Station on 17 September at 4 p.m., he hailed a cab to the university, where he settled into room 348 of Hutton House at Sir Daniel Wilson Residence (the largest and oldest all-male house on campus which, as one of two secular residences, had a significant Jewish population). In contrast to U of M, where most of the students were from Winnipeg, U of T had kids from across the country. He'd been editor of his high school paper *Etcetera* and quickly found a place penning reviews for *The Varsity* (one of several campus publications), scoring free movie tickets while honing his writing.

Soon after arriving in Toronto, Secter started frequenting gay bars, including Letros and the St Charles Tavern, and made occasional jaunts to the Roman Baths, the city's most popular gay sauna, all of which were easier to find than Winnipeg's clandestine haunts. He was never caught up in any of the police raids happening during this period nor did he hear anything about the on-campus gay bashings Heather Dean had reported. ("I was unaware of any gay activity on campus, let alone anti-gay activity," he tells me, laughing [Secter, interview, 17 December 2019].) The city offered sexual opportunities beyond anything he'd dreamed of. But as he gradually settled into his new life, he found himself craving romance.

The Inspiration for *Winter*

On 3 December, as noted in his diary, Secter began a relationship that would change the course of his life. It was the date of his first conversation with Alain, a freshman philosophy major who waited tables in the dining hall. The pair quickly became fast friends, taking in the city's cultural offerings and spending long evenings discussing creative aspirations, career goals, and (in Alain's case) girls. Secter had no interest in returning home for the summer so as the year came to a close, he proposed to Alain that they find an off-campus apartment together. That May, they moved into the top floor of a house in Rosedale, a posh neighbourhood not far from campus. Secter scored a plum summer job writing copy for an ad agency. Alain landed a more demanding and less lucrative gig painting houses. By this point, Secter's interest in Alain had taken a romantic turn. At the same time, Alain entered into a tumultuous relationship with a woman named Leora. Secter would listen patiently as Alain talked about the couple's fights. At one point Leora told Alain she thought his roommate's interest in him was more than platonic. Secter denied the allegation, but the friendship was never the same. Their plan had been to continue cohabitating through the upcoming school year, but Alain gave his notice before the summer was up and moved out. The two would occasionally cross paths on campus, but never really spoke again (Secter, interview, 14 December 2020).

Secter returned to school that fall. As he came to the end of the spring semester though, he found himself losing steam. He'd become disillusioned with his studies but didn't have another clear path to follow. While perusing the want ads in the 2 May edition of the *Toronto Star,* a curious offer caught his eye:

> 2 young men for 9 mos. caribbean expedition, navigator, some diving experience; also still & movie photographer writer. State age, experience & references. Box 4159 Star.

A young businessman named Paul Herbeerman was seeking crew (including a writer and a photographer) for a tropical voyage. Secter arranged to meet him and quickly realized his prospective employer was more adventure-seeker than entrepreneur, having only a skeleton plan and no money to fund it. If he wanted the nine-month gig the posting had promised, he'd need to help raise the cash required. Nevertheless, he agreed to join the team on the condition they increase the project's scope.

The original idea had been to take off in a trimaran that fall, heading south for warmer climates and making a documentary about the trip along the way. Secter argued for expanding their travels to Europe and Australia, believing prospective backers would have a more positive response. Hoping to tap into funds slated for Expo 67 and the country's Centennial celebrations, he suggested they screen some Canadian films along the way, at the same time as they were making one. The idea was fuzzy at best. Would they just arrive at random ports, film canisters in hand, and ask for directions to the nearest cinema? After a few trips to Ottawa to woo sponsors, it became clear to everyone that the duo lacked the necessary skills to pull off the project. With fall approaching, Secter had to decide whether he was returning to university. With no funding in place, the impossibility of the voyage sank in. Completing his degree became the easier choice.

Despite the project's failure, the overall experience was a critical juncture in Secter's creative journey. During one of the pitches he'd met Roman Kroitor, the influential documentary filmmaker who also worked for the NFB and was heading the organization's Expo 67 project. During their meeting, Kroitor asked a painfully obvious question: "Have any of you actually made a movie before?" Realizing Kroitor could be the key to bigger opportunities, Secter quickly fibbed and declared he was about to wrap production on a short. The lie failed to secure funding, but the meeting demonstrated the need for a calling card if he wanted to enter the industry. He quickly committed to making his imaginary project a reality.

The limited resources Herbeerman had cobbled together included a 16 mm camera and a basic editing setup. On 27 July, six days after the meeting, Secter's diary notes his first idea for *A Fishy Tale*: a water-themed short and possible nod to his now-dead seafaring dreams. On 1 August, he scored 300 feet of 16 mm colour film at a discounted price. Along with two actors and a pair of production assistants, Secter got to work. After a few days of hectic shooting and editing, he had his first film: *Love with the Proper Guppy*, a whimsical eight-minute silent movie about a lovesick fish, loosely based on Bizet's opera *Carmen*. (The total budget for the production, including hamburgers for the cast, was $31.88.) Ten days later he left for the Montreal International Film Festival, where he arranged a handful of private screenings for friends, including *Toronto Star* critic David Cobb, who would later write multiple articles about his work. He also sent a copy to Kroitor, but never heard back. Secter later sold the piece to CBC Television, where a proper soundtrack was added and the film was put it into regular rotation. The ramshackle process of shooting and editing proved revolutionary for Secter. "Suddenly I had a new direction in my life that became more important and compelling than sailing

Figure 7
Subway serenade: Peter Kastner and Julie Biggs in Don Owen's *Nobody Waved Good-bye*

around the world," he says. "Once I had that taste, my desire to make movies was awakened" (Secter, interview, 30 November 2020).

The Montreal festival included another pivotal moment in his journey to filmmaking: a screening of NFB director Don Owen's *Nobody Waved Good-bye*. Featuring unknown actors and improvised dialogue, Owen's groundbreaking story of youthful rebellion was only the second narrative feature produced by the NFB. Secter was astonished to see his adopted hometown on screen, something he'd never experienced outside newsreels and the odd documentary. "I recognized the streets and even some of the people," he says. "It was one of the few things I'd seen that said it was possible to make movies here" (Secter, interview, 30 November 2020).

Figure 8
Joy Ride: Peter and Julie cruising in a stolen car.

Near the end of August, Secter had his first contact with the films of the French New Wave courtesy of a two-week festival at Toronto's New Yorker Theatre. Made with handheld cameras and film stock that functioned with natural light, both developed during World War II, these works offered relevant contemporary stories at the same time they critiqued the state of their national cinema. He was also impressed that these transatlantic directors, many of whom were just a few years older than he was, had mostly launched their careers without studio support or professional training. Instead, many of the field's leading figures, including François Truffaut and Jean-Luc Godard,

Figure 9
The crew capturing the final scene in François Truffaut's *The 400 Blows*. Photo by André Dino. From filmaffinity.com.

had found their way to filmmaking by writing reviews, just as Secter had been doing. In contrast to American blockbusters, these films told the kind of intimate stories he could imagine himself making. Most importantly, perhaps, they demonstrated an accessible approach to production. "If you saw shots of a Hollywood movie set, they had these enormous cameras and hundreds of people," Secter says. "Whereas if you saw behind the scenes of a Truffaut film, you realized they were using a handheld camera and a crew of six. In terms of style and practicality, this was the kind of movie I knew I'd be able to make" (Secter, interview, 30 November 2020). Notably, Truffaut, Godard, and other French New Wave filmmakers typically shot numerous on-set stills and often used these images as part of their press material. Rather than trying to disguise the meagreness of their productions, they actively promoted it,

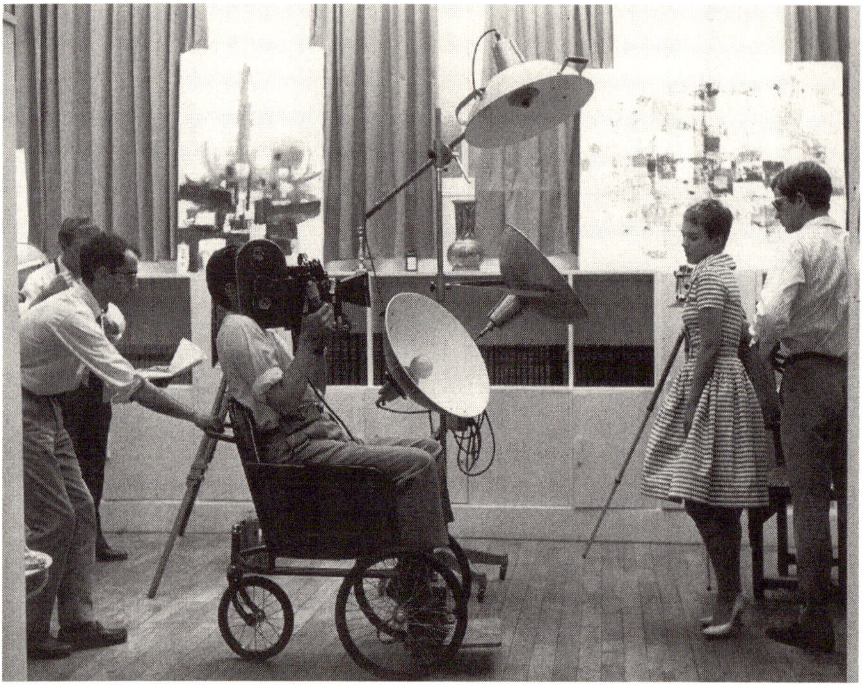

Figure 10
A low cost dolly alternative on the set of Jean-Luc Godard's *Breathless*.
Photo by Raymond Cauchetier. From Rob Baker, "Brilliant Behind the Scenes Photos of A Bout de Souffle (Breathless)," flashbak.com, 18 December 2017.

cashing in on their outsider status and inspiring a new generation of artists, including Secter, to work with what they had.

For Secter, inexperience led to a kind of blind ambition. Having read that Orson Welles made *Citizen Kane* at twenty-four, he figured he was running out of time. In September 1964, he returned to school with the goal of launching his directorial career. On 17 October he found his subject. Like generations of artists who came before, he would spin heartbreak into art. His debut film would tell the story of his relationship with Alain.

The Beginning of *Winter*

Once Secter had his subject, the process moved at warp speed. In the days after cementing his concept, he drafted a synopsis. Originally called *Doug and Peter*, Secter later changed the title to *Winter Kept Us Warm*, a line from T.S. Eliot's *The Waste Land*. He knew little about Eliot or the inspiration for the poem but felt the name captured the fleeting nature of the relationship he wanted to portray.

On 30 October, a two-hundred-word article appeared in *The Varsity* that proclaimed: "U of T student to produce movie on campus." Penned by Secter, though it didn't include a byline, it opened with the question, "Will 'the great Canadian film' be shot at U of T?" and included a call for lighting and sound technicians, writers, actors, and "Anyone who owns or can operate 16 mm movie equipment." Production, the text said, would begin in less than a month (Secter 1964). Fittingly, it was published on the same page as Secter's gushing review of *Nobody Waved Good-bye*. To anyone with filmmaking knowledge, this was clearly a team that didn't have much to start with or know enough to care. Probably better described as an advertisement, the article perfectly encapsulated the critical mix of passion and innocence Secter would need to follow his dream.

On 1 November, a few dozen aspiring actors and crew gathered in the room of Eric Rump, one of University College's residence dons (senior students and academic advisors). This initial group included Ron B. Thomson, who would eventually become the film's executive producer. According to Thomson, many attendees believed they were joining a filmmaking club. After Secter made it clear the team would be focused on *his* project, only a fraction returned for subsequent meetings. "People came and went, especially at the

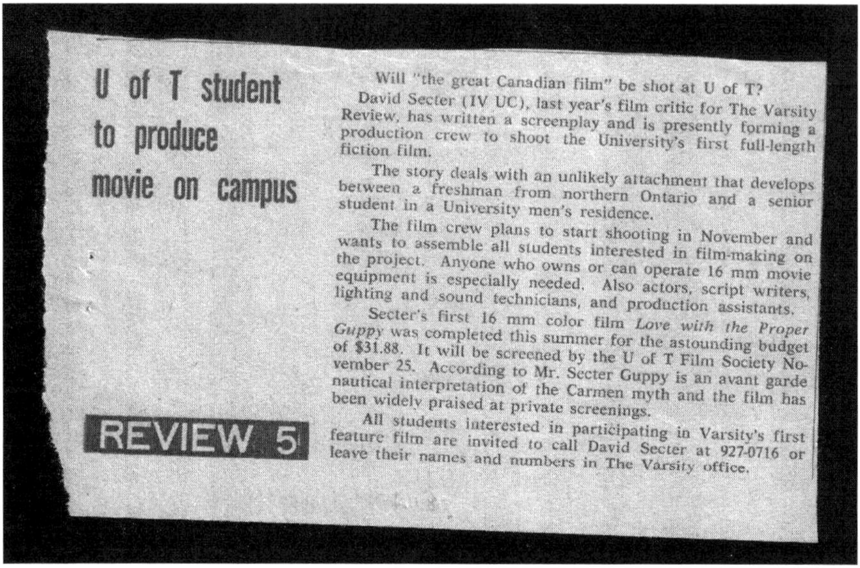

U of T student to produce movie on campus

Will "the great Canadian film" be shot at U of T?

David Secter (IV UC), last year's film critic for The Varsity Review, has written a screenplay and is presently forming a production crew to shoot the University's first full-length fiction film.

The story deals with an unlikely attachment that develops between a freshman from northern Ontario and a senior student in a University men's residence.

The film crew plans to start shooting in November and wants to assemble all students interested in film-making on the project. Anyone who owns or can operate 16 mm movie equipment is especially needed. Also actors, script writers, lighting and sound technicians, and production assistants.

Secter's first 16 mm color film *Love with the Proper Guppy* was completed this summer for the astounding budget of $31.88. It will be screened by the U of T Film Society November 25. According to Mr. Secter Guppy is an avant garde nautical interpretation of the Carmen myth and the film has been widely praised at private screenings.

All students interested in participating in Varsity's first feature film are invited to call David Secter at 927-0716 or leave their names and numbers in The Varsity office.

REVIEW 5

Figure 11
Secter's first stab at self-promotion: *Winter*'s production announcement in *The Varsity*.

beginning," Thomson says. "I think in the end we shrank to a group of around twenty, including the actors, film crew, and hangers-on" (Ron B. Thomson, interview with author, 7 December 2020). Thomson began as a jack-of-all-trades, holding the sound boom, operating the tape recorder, and hauling lights. Ultimately, he took over project administration, tracking the unpaid bills that were steadily racking up and keeping creditors at bay with money that was trickling in from various grants Secter was able to secure. (Since he handled the paperwork, Thomson retained a substantial archive relating to the production, which he complemented over time with newspaper clippings.)

It quickly became clear that the potential participants had neither the technical knowledge nor the necessary equipment to help Secter on his quest, so he approached Ryerson Polytechnic Institute (now Toronto Metropolitan University), another of the city's post-secondary institutions. Ryerson didn't have a film production program yet; York University's, which launched in 1969, was Canada's first (Feldman 2006). But it had a photography department, which offered a single third-year course in moving images. This meant a pool of students with a modicum of training and, more importantly, access to equipment that was mostly available free of charge. Secter cold-called Darryl Williams, head of the program, to ask for support. Williams pitched the students and seven or eight showed interest, though most dropped out after the first meeting when they realized the time commitment involved. In the end, only Robert Fresco and Ernest Meershoek, the film's directors of photography, stuck around. But their knowledge came in handy. Fresco had shot a handful of news items and assisted on an NFB-backed documentary short about a Southern California renaissance festival called *Pleasure Faire*. Meershoek had several years of experience as a portrait photographer under his belt. He also stepped in at the last minute to voice the cab driver's lines for the opening scene.

Paul Hoffert, the film's composer, was a U of T sciences student, but had been a professional musician for several years. In addition to regular gigs at CBC, he did music for campus theatre troupes including UC Follies, where future *Saturday Night Live* creator Lorne Michaels, then Lorne Lipowitz, got his start as a director. He agreed to work for free (as did the rest of the team) but insisted on a budget for professional musicians to ensure high-quality results. The team included Rob McConnell (trombone), Moe Koffman (flute), Eugene Amaro, (alto sax and flute), Ron Laurie (cello), Ed Bickert (guitar), Stan Zadak and Doug Willson (acoustic double bass), and Ed Thigpen and Stan Perry (drums). "The music was perhaps the only element that was done with really great production quality," Hoffert says. "I'll always be grateful to David for allowing me to use a proper recording studio and musicians. Because it was so well done, the film was an inflection point in my life" (Paul Hoffert, interview with author, 19 November 2020). Hoffert went on to score dozens of films and TV shows, including another landmark queer Canadian work, Richard Benner's 1977 film *Outrageous!*

One of the score's most distinctive elements is a riff on "Tuoll on mun kultani (Far Away Is My Love)," a popular Finnish folk song. Secter wanted to weave elements of each actor's background into their characters. During an early conversation, Henry Tarvainen had shared a record of Finnish folk music (his parents were immigrants) and Secter decided to incorporate the song into the film and Tarvainen's cultural background into his role. Hoffert stripped the composition to its elements and then rearranged it, turning some notes upside down and playing other parts backward. This new rendition serves as Peter's theme music throughout the film and the original version appears when Doug plays it on the guitar, a talent given to the character because of John Labow's existing abilities.

Casting

The early meetings secured some crew but failed to produce any actors. Michaels was initially cast as Nick, one of Doug's friends. He later backed out, though he offered some assistance with the script. (The role ultimately went to Jack Messinger.) Secter found each of the film's four leads in a slightly different way. None involved an audition as there wasn't sufficient time or interest to warrant that process. "There was a degree of beggars can't be choosers," Secter says. "A limited number of people were ready to put in that much time for nothing. There was a certain amount of luck involved because I was taking them on spec, they were taking me on spec, and the whole project was a wild dream with no reasonable expectation that it would turn out as well as it did" (Secter, interview, 26 May 2021).

Janet Amos was the first to get involved. (Secter noted in his diary on 29 October that she would play Sandra.) He had approached her on a recommendation from Robert Gill, artistic director of Hart House Theatre, who had cast her in several plays. "He said that Gill had called me the best actress on campus," Amos laughs. "I don't know if that was true or not because he was always very generous in his assessment of people, but that's what David told me" (Janet Amos, interview with author, 20 November 2020). Whether it was truth or flattery, Amos agreed to be in the film. Tarvainen joined shortly after, also on a recommendation. Like Amos, he was a regular in campus theatre productions. Secter had never seen him perform but cast him after one conversation, based largely on his enthusiasm. Joy Fielding (then Joy Tepperman) had also appeared in a number of shows, primarily at Women's College Theatre and Hart House. She thinks she learned about the film from Amos but can't clearly recall. What she does remember is that she approached Secter directly after hearing about the project. He explained that the story focused on the two male leads (no mention of the gay subject matter). She knew Amos had been cast as one character's girlfriend, so she proposed to play the other's. It was a bold move because, at that point, the role didn't exist. Secter had imagined Doug as a burgeoning womanizer with several minor flings on the go. In an effort to secure a part, Fielding convinced him the film would function better if it were about two couples. Since her role wasn't part of the original plot, Secter advised her she would need to have a hand in developing her scenes. "I can't imagine the film would have worked as well as it did if we didn't have that Doug/Bev relationship," Secter says. "She was absolutely right" (Secter, interview, 30 November 2020).

The part of Doug turned out to be the most challenging to cast. Secter initially had two actors agree to the role, both of whom dropped out when they realized the commitment involved and the unlikelihood of the project ever being finished. He had seen Labow in a Hart House production of *Look Back in Anger* the previous spring, but wasn't thinking about making a film at that point. He doesn't remember the selection process but noted in his diary that he was considering several people as of 16 November. Two days later, he confirmed Labow and they began rehearsals with Tarvainen for the library scene that afternoon. As with the other roles, Secter didn't have particularly firm criteria for the part. "I just needed someone who would be believable as the popular guy on campus," he says. "I didn't have the luxury of looking for a specific type. It was just about who I could con into participating" (Secter, interview, 26 May 2021).

University Permissions

Once he had assembled his team, Secter needed license from the university. That a feature film had never been shot on campus was both a help and a hindrance in this regard. Specifically, it meant there was no centralized system for getting the necessary authorizations. Instead, they had to work on a location-by-location basis, sometimes making inquiries the same day or even, as Secter says, "shooting based on anticipated permits" (i.e., without formal agreement). The first location they sought was the interior of the residences, for which they easily got approval from the house dons, several of whom were part of the initial meetings. The next step was to approach the higher-ups for access to the public areas of campus. Secter submitted a five-page treatment outlining the story and required locations to Douglas LePan, principal of University College, the part of campus where they would be shooting. The summary made the film's already toned-down gay element even less obvious. Nevertheless, on 30 October, the same day his announcement ran in *The Varsity*, LePan declined their request, noting concern over the homoerotic aspects. Although the story's queerness was very subtly rendered, it was easy for LePan to spot since he was a closeted gay man. (A two-time Governor General's Award winner and officer of the Order of Canada, LePan tentatively came out in 1990, eight years before his death, when he published a slim volume of largely gay love poetry called *Far Voyages.*) How permission was ultimately obtained, no one seems to remember. But thanks to the persistent support of a number of professors and academic advisors, *Winter* somehow got the green light.

The Script

After assembling his team, Secter was ready to shoot. He was, however, missing a key ingredient: the script. Some members of the team pressed him for one but according to Secter, there was no time to write it. The story arc spanned three different seasons, which meant they had to start shooting before the snow fell. Since it was already the beginning of November, that deadline might be days away. Also, use of the university locations was contingent on Secter being a student. If he returned the following year after graduating, the administration might charge an exorbitant fee or refuse access altogether. "There was a real sense of urgency in getting started," Secter says. "I knew if I didn't make this movie now, I might never make it at all. Some of the directors who inspired me used on-camera improvisation. It would be nice to say I was following their lead, but the decision to work without a script came down to mix of necessity and procrastination" (Secter, interview, 26 May 2021). In the end, there was never a complete script at any point in the process. "We were always scrambling to write a scene just before shooting it," he says. "I didn't really know how the movie would finish until we'd already shot nearly all of it" (Secter, interview, 26 May 2021). Secter, the actors, and fellow students John Clute and Ian Porter (who also appears in the cast party scene) developed the dialogue, frequently through improvisation and often minutes before the shoot. In an ironic twist, Secter authored an entirely different version of the screenplay, long since lost, during a creative writing course he took that year as part of his degree.

Funding

By mid-November, Secter had found his cast and crew, arranged a basic shooting set-up, and scored a bit of film stock on the cheap (partially used reels from other production companies, known as "short ends"). He had a synopsis, an improvisational shooting style, and boundless creative energy. But he still didn't have any money. The university's Students' Administrative Council initially offered $750, but according to Secter this was positioned as a loan and came with the right to control distribution. (The council later committed a few hundred dollars with no strings attached.) He received an additional $800 from University College, which was enough to get started but far from what was needed. The goal was to raise $5,000. In the end, the film was produced for just under $8,000 (Hicklin 1964).

He knew that potential backers would want a preview of the work before agreeing to fund it, so he set out to shoot a teaser that would trigger the flow of cash. On 22 November they tackled their first scene: Doug and Peter's meeting in the library (Secter 1965). Filming started at 3:00 p.m. and was expected to wrap by midnight; they didn't finish until 7:00 a.m. "That was a learning experience for us all as we worked out the issues with lighting, sound, and camera angles," Thomson recalls. "As we were packing up, we heard an ambulance with its siren pass by on Queen's Park Crescent. We were along one of the main routes to the various hospitals south of the university and we realized how lucky we'd been that none had gone through overnight" (Thomson, interview). The group planned to pair this section with Doug and Peter's earlier interaction in the dining room to give a hint of the story and, as Secter says, flaunt the film's "big production values" (Secter, interview, 30 November 2020). This next scene was shot 8 December. Despite being a considerably bigger setup with over a hundred extras, Secter had an even smaller crew; a good number of people had dropped out after that first surprise all-nighter. The library scene was underscored with awkwardness ("somehow or other we were able to salvage it," Secter says [Secter, interview, 30 November 2020]) and

Figure 12
After dinner in the library: Doug tries to make amends.

the dining room section was rife with lighting problems and uneven audio. Nevertheless, with these two scenes shot and edited, they went in search of capital to support the production. Secter's leap from a single self-produced short to a fully funded feature was always going to be an unlikely gamble. Major funders, both public and private, want to see clear creative ability and demonstrated production capacity before they pitch in. But as Secter points out, because the Canadian film industry was still in its infancy, the rules had yet to be written.

The film's breakneck schedule meant the team had to forge ahead without any confirmed funding. They applied to the Canada Council for the Arts, the Ontario Arts Council, the NFB, Toronto City Council, and several private production companies. Ultimately, none of the anticipated cash came through.

Figure 13
First meeting: Peter serving food in the dining hall.

(Secter's diary notes that the NFB rejection came 4 March and Toronto City Council's arrived 25 March.) Since the equipment was largely borrowed and the team was working for free, the main costs would be film stock, processing, and editing. Fortunately, there was Film House, the Toronto lab and post-production facility founded by entrepreneur Bob Crone earlier that year. Crone agreed to support the project by allowing them to run up a debt. (*Winter* was the first project Film House took on, so perhaps the fledgling facility was more generous than it would have been had Secter approached them later [Eichhorn 1997].) "By and large, people there were impressed by what we were

Figure 14
Secter's first shot: prepping for day number one in the library.
The Varsity, date unknown.

doing, so they cut us some slack," Secter says. "They probably didn't intend to let us build up as big a debt as we did. I have to give them a lot of credit. I don't think we could have made the film without them" (Secter, interview, 30 November 2020).

Shooting

Shooting was originally slated to last through April. An unplanned break was added in late March to accommodate final exams, with the team returning in May to complete key scenes before everyone went home for the summer. With the need to work around everyone's lectures, labs, and assignments, scheduling was a perpetual challenge. Most shots were done in a single take; there wasn't enough time or film stock to experiment.

In November 1965, a few months after the film wrapped, Secter documented the team's struggles in a first-person account for the *Globe and Mail*. Production crises, he wrote, included "1,200 feet of negative lost and never found, the soundtrack on several scenes accidentally erased, and one broken leg (actor Jack Messinger's) that had to be written into the script" (Secter 1965). Capturing Doug and Peter's pivotal romp in the quad was a particular challenge. The scene called for sunny skies, falling snow, and an unsullied patch of powder for them to frolic in. "The crew was on twenty-four-hour alert for five weeks with a hot-line to Malton's forecasters (the local weather station) until the perfect conditions occurred, unannounced," Secter says. "I woke everyone at 4:00 a.m. and the once-only scene was shot at dawn with six cameras hidden around the quad" (Secter 1965).

Despite these challenges, Secter remained mostly calm throughout the process. "He was relatively easy to work with, as long as you realized it was his show," Thomson says. "However, he took a lot of advice from the people who worked on the dialogue, including the four main actors, and the camera crew who could suggest angles and lighting strategies. People chipped in their ideas on how to solve certain problems, and David was willing to take those and incorporate them into his own design" (Thomson, interview).

He also had a light touch with the actors. "He didn't direct too much," Amos recalls. "He was very concerned with the technical things going on. But he wasn't trying to shape your acting particularly. You'd have a little rehearsal and he'd give some suggestions. He'd be watching very hard and listening, trying to make the story work or rewrite some lines. But he wasn't a 'director' director, pushing people the way some of them do. He just let you do your thing" (Amos, interview). Fielding adds: "He just sort of told us what he wanted in scenes and then we more or less improvised our own dialogue and wrote it down. We would rehearse a bit and then David would say it was okay, and we would film it. I don't remember feeling it was strange. I just thought that was the way you made a film. When you're young, you don't necessarily question things as much. You just go with it because you're fearless in a way you aren't when you're older" (Fielding, interview).

Similarly, locations were sourced as filming progressed. The library scenes were shot after hours and the dining hall sections were captured between mealtimes. The winter carnival section was done guerrilla style. The cast party took place in the basement flat Secter rented after parting ways with Alain. For Sandra's place, they used the apartment of a cast member's sister. Other interiors (various bars, the Finnish sauna) were filmed with a quick agreement from the venue. Exteriors, including the front of the O'Keefe Centre and the walk along Yonge Street were done on the fly. Working largely with borrowed equipment meant they would sometimes realize a critical item was missing on the day of a shoot. More than once they snuck into the equipment bay at Ryerson to snag something after hours, hoping to return it before it was missed. The learning curve was steep, but the finished work reflects the team's growth. As they largely shot in sequence, with the exception of the early driving scenes, which were done in May, viewers can witness technical errors diminishing and performances solidifying over the course of the film.

Press Coverage during the Production

Among the many things that make *Winter* unusual is the substantial amount of press it received during the production process. The novelty of a student-led feature caught the attention of both local and national media, coverage Secter actively sought in the hopes of securing additional backers. Having written a few articles for the *Toronto Star*, he had a sense of how to pitch a story. "It wasn't a hard sell," Secter laughs. "Our production was so paltry it was news. There was definitely a sense that we were delusional college kids who thought we were going to make a movie worth seeing" (Secter, interview, 26 May 2021).

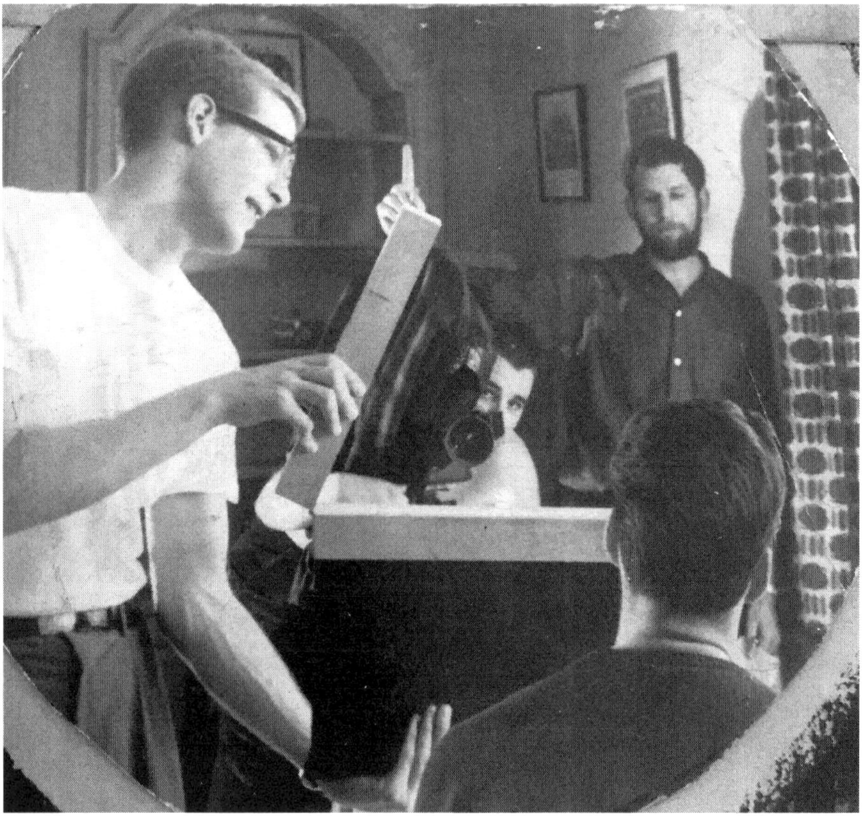

Figure 15
Double duty: Henry Tarvainen helms the clapperboard. Photographer unknown, courtesy of David Secter.

21 November, the day before shooting commenced, the *Globe and Mail* published an interview with Secter. He was predictably guarded about the subject matter; his theme, he said, was that "friendship, like snow, is brilliant but ephemeral." When asked about the production, he was surprisingly cocky, saying that they had "no shortage of film-makers or philanthropists ready to back

Figure 16
Following Truffaut's lead: preparing to shoot from a moving car. Photographer unknown, courtesy of David Secter.

the production" (Hicklin 1964), which was either a bold speculation on funds to come, a covert pitch to potential investors, or both. On 15 January, he told McKenzie Porter of the *Toronto Telegram* that he had shared rushes with Twentieth Century Theatres, Lawrence Productions, and Chetwynd Films, all of whom said the picture "showed promise of becoming a commercial success"

(Porter 1965). Secter did in fact contact all three companies, but none of them were interested; allusions to the work's mainstream potential were another fabrication aimed at drumming up investors (Secter, interview, 26 May 2021). Shortly after, in the *Toronto Star*, he bemoaned a lack of assistance, noting "all kinds of moral support" but no concrete funds (Cobb 1965).

The media coverage failed to secure investment. Instead, it resulted in something more valuable: international attention. On 27 April, Secter got a letter from the Commonwealth Film Festival in Cardiff. News of the project had spread across the Atlantic and they asked him to submit the film for consideration. According to Secter, he initially didn't reply (Cobb 1965). The film was far from finished and there no was cash in sight to complete it. A month later, the festival began ramping up pressure with phone calls and telegrams, indicating they hoped to present the work as their opening night film. The only edited material was the seven-minute sample Secter had shown prospective funders, so he mailed a copy of that. 16 July he received confirmation it had been selected. "To be candid, I still don't know why they took it," he says. "They didn't see much of the movie. It hadn't been made at that point so it just seemed like an incredible leap of faith" (Secter, interview, 30 March 2021).[1]

Secter had intended to edit the film himself. The offer from Cardiff forced a change of plans. By mid-July, he had a three-hour rough cut (more aptly described as an aggregate of all potentially useable footage). Faced with a looming deadline, he brought editor Michael Foytényi on board based on a recommendation from his old acting teacher John Hirsch, who had worked with Foytényi at CBC. Foytényi quickly realized the task was too large to tackle on his own and called in George Appleby. (Although Appleby is credited as associate editor, he completed 35–40 per cent of the film on his own, according to Secter.) The work began at the now-shuttered 354 Jarvis Street CBC Building, later moving to Film House. The pair mostly worked in separate editing suites, with Secter bouncing back and forth and Paul Hoffert dropping in to watch sequences and compose music based on what he saw.

With what they'd shot so far, Secter had a rough story arc but no concrete ending. He considered a few alternatives for Doug including reconciling with Bev and a new appreciation for Artie, Iain Ewing's character. None of these seemed right as they pulled focus from the central point of the film. Instead, he opted for the version we see: Doug alone in the library reading *The Waste Land*, struck by, as Secter says, "the subtle recognition he's got a lot of things to figure out" (Secter, interview, 30 March 2021). The cast and crew returned to set in July and captured the final scenes. Shooting officially wrapped 21 August 1965.

Secter continued doing interviews through post-production, still hoping to raise additional funds. His tone in these later pieces is dramatically different. In earlier articles, he'd gushed about the frenzied interest of financial backers and the film's potential as a cinematic cash cow. Now, he was flogging the paltriness of the production and bemoaning the lack of support. Speaking with the *Winnipeg Free Press*, he proudly dubbed it "the lowest budget feature film ever made in Canada." He also made fairly direct mention of the subject matter, saying, "People can read into it what they want. I suppose homosexual overtones could be seen in the boys' friendship – they can be seen anywhere I suppose" (*Winnipeg Free Press*, 1965). Shortly before Cardiff, he did another interview with David Cobb for the *Toronto Star*, where he discussed his continued financial struggles and the "indifference of the NFB." (The article also quotes Gordon Burwash, the board's acting director of English production, saying the NFB had watched an incomplete version of the film and "it was terribly difficult to judge it in that form, but the truth was that we weren't that impressed with it and gently said so" [Cobb 1965].) In addition to tracking the film's financial struggles, these articles offer a record of Secter's learning process. From his initial announcement in *The Varsity* through the final pieces pre-Cardiff, we watch him go from passionate yet somewhat clueless to grounded and slightly jaded. They also offer a window into how the rest of his career would go. Secter would never become a filmmaker who worked

Figure 17
Secter at the camera. *The Varsity*, date unknown.

within established systems. Instead, he would continue to find ways around conventional gatekeepers, both in how he made his work and how he shared it with the public.

Screenings

The journey to Cardiff had much of the same madcap energy as the production. Unable to secure travel funding, Secter had booked space for himself and director of photography Robert Fresco on a charter flight alongside Toronto's Balmy Beach rugby team, who were headed to Edinburgh for a match. From there, the duo would catch a connecting flight to London, rent a car, and drive the rest of the way. Editing continued until the last possible moment. The afternoon of their departure, Secter and Fresco packed their bags, hailed a cab to Film House where Thomson handed off the canister, and continued to the airport just in time to catch their flight. At that point only Thomson had seen the completed film, which he'd watched once through to make sure the print wasn't damaged. Navigating the narrow back roads through the English countryside from London to Cardiff took considerably longer than expected and they arrived at the cinema with the public already seated. Breathlessly, they handed the print to the projectionist, and installed themselves at the back of the theatre, ready to watch their film for the first time.

Secter's memory of the screening is fuzzy. "I'm sure I was nervous. I'm sure I cringed, as I still do in certain places when I watch the film," he says. "There are some things I'll never be able to fix that will always bother me. Some missing sound effects that didn't make it into the mix and moments where the audio is out of sync" (Secter, interview, 26 May 2021). Hoping to build on the attention from the festival, Secter and Fresco stayed in the UK for another two weeks, arranging private viewings and even scoring a meeting with reps from

Figure 18
Just under the wire: Secter handing the film to the projectionist in Cardiff. Uncredited photograph, *Western Mail* newspaper, 14 September 1965.

the BBC. They returned to Toronto slightly dejected, without any confirmed screenings dates or distribution offers.

Beyond the lack of opportunities for the film, Secter had a bigger problem: the substantial debt accrued while making it. Hoping to generate some cash, he approached the New Yorker Theatre, where he had first encountered the

French New Wave, to arrange a run. They declined, stating that the film, especially its sound, wasn't high enough quality. The following day, 26 October, he booked the cinema at the Royal Ontario Museum for a two-week stint. It began 6 December with a press screening, which was also the first time the cast had seen the finished work. "Everybody was a little surprised that it turned out," Secter laughs. "I think they were pleased that all this time they'd put into it resulted in something worth showing" (Secter, interview, 26 May 2021). Being forced to self-distribute turned out to be a blessing in disguise. Had the film played at a commercial cinema they would have seen only a fraction of the profits. Instead, they recouped enough money by the end of the run to pay off the remaining production costs. That same month, he sent a copy to the NFB in the hopes the organization might distribute it.

In order to screen the work publicly, Secter needed clearance from the Ontario Film Review Board (the provincial agency tasked with assigning ratings). After a near rejection, the film squeaked by with a "Restricted" designation. The team found out just how close they had come to a refusal via Thomson's mother, who played bridge with a woman from the board. "My mother mentioned that I had worked on *Winter Kept Us Warm* and the woman gave her a long stare, before exclaiming 'that film!'" Thomson recalls. "She said they had a great deal of difficulty passing it for viewing and were on the edge of banning it. In the end, since it was only showing for a limited run and was mainly geared to university students, they finally agreed to let it through, but gave it the highest restriction they could" (Thomson, interview).

In January 1966, the film began a six-week stint at the Pace Cinema in Winnipeg, followed by two weeks at Toronto's Elektra Theatre. During the run at the Elektra, Secter finally received a response to his NFB query. Lucille Bishop, the board's distribution agent, had submitted *Winter* as Canada's entry to the Cannes Festival's *Semaine de la Critique*, where *Seul ou avec d'autres* had also played. To call screening at Cannes the fulfilment of a dream isn't quite right. It would be more accurate to dub it the joyful punch line to a long-running

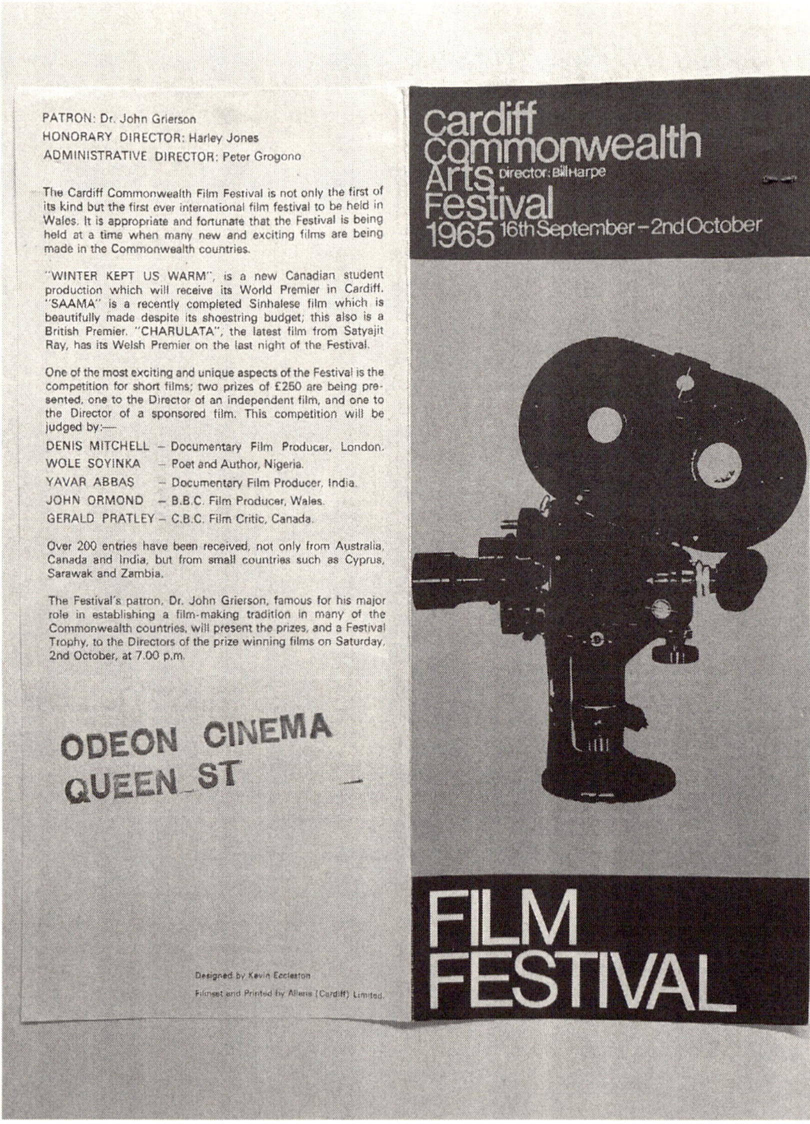

PATRON: Dr. John Grierson

HONORARY DIRECTOR: Harley Jones

ADMINISTRATIVE DIRECTOR: Peter Grogono

The Cardiff Commonwealth Film Festival is not only the first of its kind but the first ever international film festival to be held in Wales. It is appropriate and fortunate that the Festival is being held at a time when many new and exciting films are being made in the Commonwealth countries.

"WINTER KEPT US WARM", is a new Canadian student production which will receive its World Premier in Cardiff. "SAAMA" is a recently completed Sinhalese film which is beautifully made despite its shoestring budget; this also is a British Premier. "CHARULATA", the latest film from Satyajit Ray, has its Welsh Premier on the last night of the Festival.

One of the most exciting and unique aspects of the Festival is the competition for short films; two prizes of £250 are being presented, one to the Director of an independent film, and one to the Director of a sponsored film. This competition will be judged by:—

DENIS MITCHELL – Documentary Film Producer, London.
WOLE SOYINKA – Poet and Author, Nigeria.
YAVAR ABBAS – Documentary Film Producer, India.
JOHN ORMOND – B.B.C. Film Producer, Wales.
GERALD PRATLEY – C.B.C. Film Critic, Canada.

Over 200 entries have been received, not only from Australia, Canada and India, but from small countries such as Cyprus, Sarawak and Zambia.

The Festival's patron, Dr. John Grierson, famous for his major role in establishing a film-making tradition in many of the Commonwealth countries, will present the prizes, and a Festival Trophy, to the Directors of the prize winning films on Saturday, 2nd October, at 7.00 p.m.

ODEON CINEMA
QUEEN ST

Designed by Kevin Eccleston
Filmset and Printed by Allens (Cardiff) Limited.

Cardiff Commonwealth Arts Festival 1965
Director: Bill Harpe
16th September – 2nd October

FILM FESTIVAL

Figure 19
Commonwealth Film Festival Program, 1965.

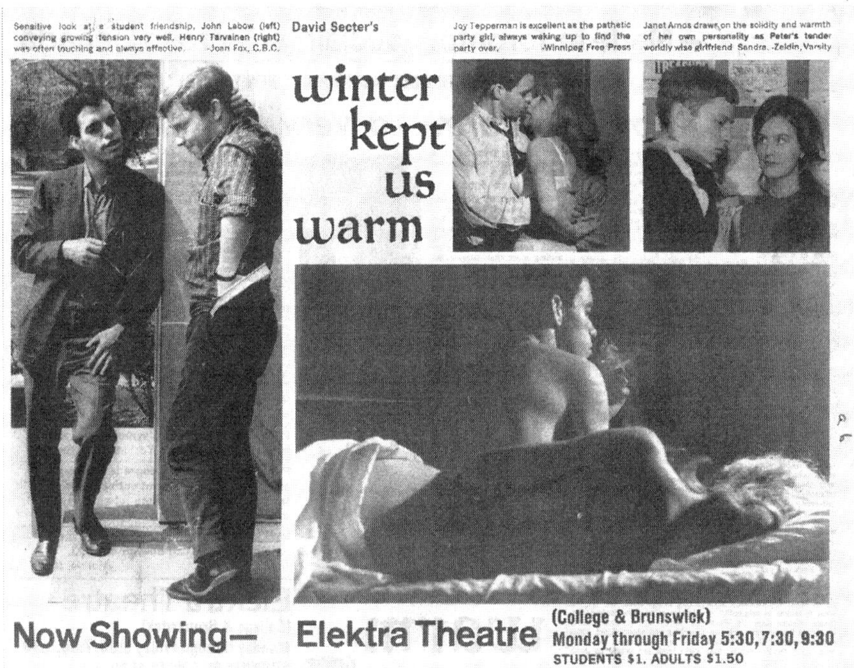

Figure 20
Sex sells: flyer for *Winter*'s run at the Elektra Theatre, Toronto.

joke. "At times, when things were really miserable on set and we didn't know how we were going to make it through, we'd say, 'Next year at Cannes we'll laugh about this,'" Secter recalls. "I suppose it was a goal from the get-go, but probably not a realistic one" (Secter, interview, 26 May 2021). This time around, the Canadian government covered Secter's travel. He got to party with celebrities and dine with Sophia Loren (that year's jury president). "Somehow I ended up at the table of ten or twelve that she was at," Secter says. "She was very gracious, making a point of talking to everyone there and we exchanged a few words. So yes, I can actually say we broke bread together" (Secter, interview, 26 May 2021).

During the run at the Royal Ontario Museum, Michael Craig, a fellow U of T student, approached Secter with the intention of helping to get the film shown. (Craig had expressed interest in the project early on, but quickly dropped out.) Over the next year and a half, Craig secured showings with university film societies across the continent, the same type of group that had triggered Secter's interest in cinema. UK critic Richard Roud, who was gay, though discreet about his sexuality at the time, had written a glowing review for the influential journal *Sight and Sound* after Cannes. He later championed the film at festivals where he worked as a programmer and booked screenings in London, Sydney, Melbourne, and elsewhere. The Montreal International Film Festival, where Secter had seen *Nobody Waved Good-bye*, also screened the work in 1966, where it scored a special jury prize "in recognition of its ambitious young film-maker, and for his great sensibility and lack of pretentiousness" (Ferry 1966). In late 1967, the film finally found a distributor, New York's fledgling Film-Makers' Cooperative. FMC secured a six-week run at the New Cinema Playhouse, the venue specializing in experimental films where many of Warhol's works had played, and a stint in Los Angeles. Screening in two major US cities helped generate additional critical attention for the work. It also set up major expectations for what Secter would do next.

Differences between the Synopsis and the Finished Work

Secter wrote several synopses for the film, only two of which survive: a concise one-page outline sent to funders and a detailed five-page version used to plan shooting. The most notable differences between these early write-ups and the final work are the queer elements. The one-page version concludes with the lines: "Doug must resign himself to the fact that the friendship is over, but at least he has discovered the depth and significance a relationship can have. The friendship is as scintillating yet as brief as the season that accompanies it … Doug and Peter find that sparkling something, that something which is as fleeting as the snow." Here, Secter's description makes it difficult to interpret the film as anything other than a budding romance.

The longer version includes a scene-by-scene plan and differs on a number of key plot points. One is the play performed by Peter and Sandra. Originally, they are cast in Robert Anderson's *Tea and Sympathy*, the story of a male student facing accusations of homosexuality, later adapted by Vincente Minnelli for the screen. Anderson's work would have been a much better *mise en abyme* for the film. Instead, Secter opted for Henrik Ibsen's *Ghosts*, since the work was in the public domain and there would be no need to secure the rights for the script. That said, Peter does recite a few lines from Shakespeare's *Richard II* during the bedroom hangover scene, a text often interpreted as a gay love story, although Secter included it without knowing this reading of the script.

A second key difference happens after the winter carnival. The original draft has Peter injure his shoulder during the game, leading to a much more explicit post-match exchange: "the boys all retire to the showers where they joke, splash cold water on one another, and celebrate. This is Doug's gift to Peter – the camaraderie and laughter. As Doug washes down Peter's back and bandages his shoulder, we see Peter's gift to Doug – a new sensitivity and commitment. When the boys go off for the post-game ritual at a nearby pub, Doug says that he and Peter will be along in a minute. We move in for a three-second freeze shot of Peter's head and torso with Doug's hand on his shoulder and Peter looking up with complete rapport."

It's impossible to know exactly how this would have been rendered on film. On the page, the sexual spark is impossible to miss and the mutual chemistry is clear. In contrast, the attraction on screen often feels one-sided, with Doug interested in Peter but not the other way around. There are, however, a few points that do hint at a shared attraction: the playful slap on the

Figure 21
"Have you ever wished that you could see yourself through somebody else's eyes?"

arm outside the record store, the backstage meeting where Peter says, "He plays my father," and the moment in the springtime montage with Sandra when Peter writes Doug's initials next to his own in a heart on the cannon, an obvious phallic symbol.

The final key difference is in how the story ends. As mentioned, Secter wasn't initially sure how the film would conclude. But his early writings contained the basic building blocks. The synopsis sees Peter and Sandra consummate their relationship prior to opening night. When Peter tells Doug, his friend congratulates him, as opposed to the film, where this admission spells

Figure 22
Boys will be boys: shower horseplay.

the end of their relationship. Instead, the big blow-up is when Peter tells Doug that he and Bev can't attend the cast party. Weeks later, Doug is alone in his room, surrounded by reminders of the friendship and unable to concentrate. Instead of going to the library, he rushes to find Peter, and they take one final walk together, though things have clearly changed. It's a less dramatic end to the friendship, more like a gradual change of seasons than the volcanic eruption we see in the film. As with the shower scene, it positions the interest as mutual, whereas the film places Doug at the centre of the story by having him undergo the biggest transformation.

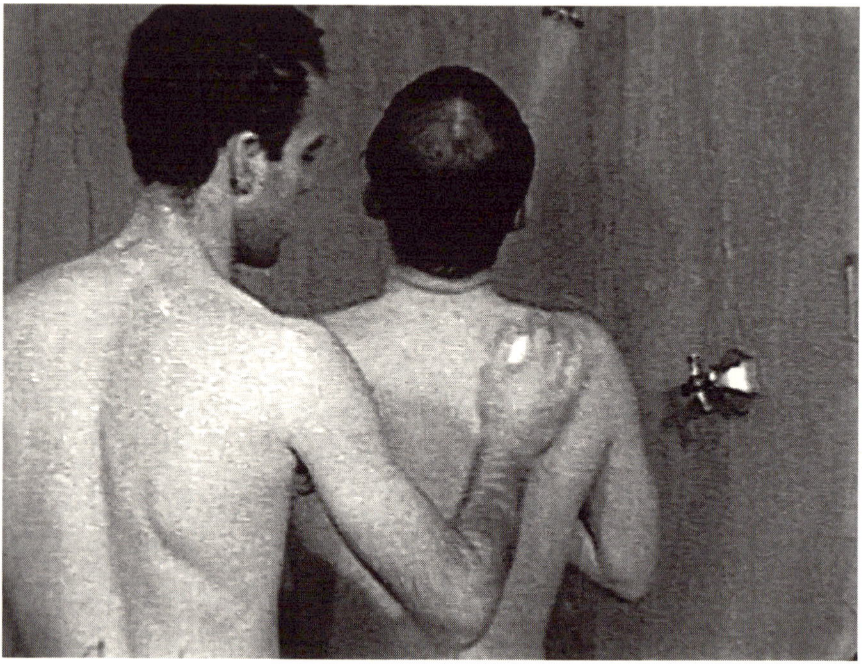

Figure 23
Sparks fly: Doug washes Peter's back in the shower.

In all three of these cases, the gay element is much less obvious on screen than in Secter's early conceptions, a decision driven by both the context of production and his hopes for presentation. Secter was creating the work at a time when homosexuality was still a crime in both Canada and the US. He was working on a university campus, an environment just as homophobic as the broader culture, if not more so. As I will discuss in chapter 4, he wasn't working within a queer community the way queer artists usually did. Instead, he was collaborating with a team of straight people at a straight institution, and so he had to consider the ramifications if the project were to "come out."

Also, Secter's ambition was to make a commercially viable film that could be shown in major theatre chains rather than being relegated to art house cinemas. At the time, mainstream North American film had no explicitly queer works, so Secter rendered his story with the same caution that previous generations of filmmakers had – with an important modification. Whether their sexualities were overtly or covertly presented, queer characters prior to this time were nearly always evil, forced to suffer, or both. While Doug does go through a transformation at the end of the film, he's not arrested, blackmailed, or beaten up to get there. Nor does he have any designs on killing Peter or Sandra. This gentler approach wasn't always the plan, however. Though it's not referenced in the synopses, Secter's original vision was somewhat closer to the tradition of queer filmmaking that preceded him. In the same diary entry where he announces that his relationship with Alain will be the film's subject, Secter contemplates portraying Doug's interest as a borderline dangerous obsession, mimicking the unsettling vibe of *The Servant*, Joseph Losey's 1963 film about a butler's fixation on his handsome employer, starring the still-closeted Dirk Bogarde. In the end, it became a largely sweet though unarticulated crush. Secter's decision to render the queer elements this way ensured the work could be seen at the time. But, as I will outline in the following chapter, in the longer term this approach also meant it would become challenging for queer audiences in the future to recognize the relationship for what it was.

Keeping Secrets from the Cast

While Secter's choice to hide the film's queerness from the university is no surprise, the fact he kept it secret from the cast is an odd quirk of *Winter*'s production history. Whether it was his cautious take on the plot or, as Matthew Hays notes, the fact that gay film didn't really exist, Secter's collaborators were largely in the dark about the film's true subject matter (Hays 2015). Ron B. Thomson, who, like Secter, lived on campus, points to an additional reason:

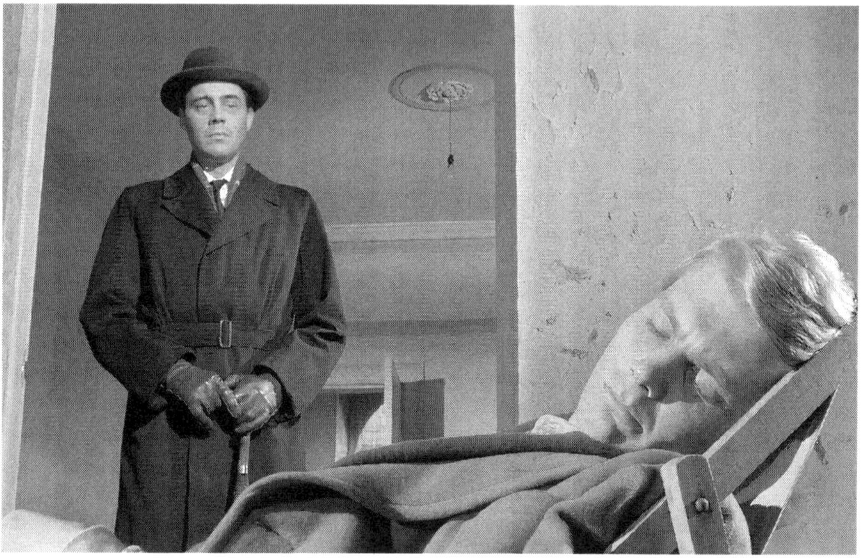

Figure 24
Although his film had a different tone, Secter still mimicked certain shots from Joseph Losey's *The Servant*. Here, Hugo (Dirk Bogarde) stares longingly at a sleeping Tony (James Fox), much like the bedroom scene in *Winter*.

"No one in residence talked openly about homosexuality," he says. "It was generally understood that you didn't label another person as gay, not even as a joke" (Thomson, interview).

Speaking in *The Best of Secter & the Rest of Secter*, John Labow, Henry Tarvainen, and Joy Fielding all claimed they had no idea what was going on. "You have a male bonding thing that has a physical component to it," Labow says during the conversation. "Closeness, affection, whatever you want to call it. Now it's homoerotic, but then it wasn't." Janet Amos recalls a conversation with Secter about the film in the 1990s. Her son Joe had seen a screening at the university (not knowing his mother had been part of it) and was discussing it with her after the fact. "He thought it was really good except that it sort of drifted off at the end," Amos says. "I was speaking with David about that later. He laughed and said that at the time, he wasn't quite clear about it either. He hadn't yet made the leap to fully acknowledging himself as a gay person, so in a way both he and the film were unresolved" (Amos, interview). Although the cast claimed to know nothing, Secter's intentions came through in their work. Bev is the only character who broaches the subject, first after Doug plays the Finnish song he'd learned on the guitar for Peter ("Why do you do so much for Peter?") and again more directly when she hints at an affair between the boys ("If I didn't know you better I'd swear you and Peter were …"), a line Fielding dropped in during an improvised script development session. "I just thought, as a girl, seeing this relationship between the two guys, I would probably say that he seems more interested in his friend than he does in me," she says. "I didn't think of it as a real accusation of homosexuality. It was more Bev asking the question to be reassured that Doug is still interested in her" (Fielding, interview).

Labow's assertion of ignorance is probably the strangest, since much of the homoerotic tension rests on his performance. Labow died in 2017, so I was unable to discuss the role with him. But in a 1982 interview with Thomas Waugh, he remembered no discussion of the gay theme, understanding the film as a story of heterosexual male friendship. Paul Hoffert also recalls a conversation with Labow around 2010. "He said David's direction to him was that Doug was feeling uncomfortable in how he was relating to women and has now discovered a new best friend," Hoffert recalls. "As an actor, he said he was never directed to have or personally contemplated any homosexual undertones" (Hoffert, interview).

According to Secter, his direction to Labow around the issue of sexuality wasn't overt, but it was hardly covert: "I would say things about Doug finding himself attracted to Peter more than he thought possible," Secter recalls. "John interpreted what I was saying in a less sexual way than I intended. But subconsciously or otherwise, he was getting it. It's there on film. If you see how

Figure 25
Secter added a part in the film where Doug plays guitar to take advantage of John Labow's existing abilities.

he looks at Peter and the way he looks at Bev, it's clear he knew the difference" (Secter, interview, 26 May 2021).

Secter and Labow remained friends for decades after the film, so they had numerous opportunities to discuss the work. According to Secter, Labow always claimed he didn't think Doug was gay or that his interest in Peter represented a shift in his sexuality. Instead, he saw Doug as feeling frustrated with the banality of life and his other relationships, and finding himself drawn to someone with a radically different experience and outlook that offered a chance to discuss topics he couldn't talk about with other people.

The cast's ignorance about the film's subject matter reveals two things. Firstly, it shows that Secter's approach succeeded. He created a queer work in a context where such a thing was nearly impossible and did so without the knowledge of the people participating. Secondly, it reflects the nature of gay life during that same period. As Secter told me, "gay" wasn't really a word people said and accusations of homosexuality were considered so extreme they almost never came up. If the cast had even a hint of what was going on, the social order of the day would have prohibited them addressing it.

The Sequel that Never Was

In the late 1980s, Secter had hoped to make a follow-up to *Winter*. Set in 1990 and tentatively called *Memory and Desire* (another line from *The Waste Land*), the film would have tracked the lives of the four main characters in the twenty-five years since the original. In the story, both couples have tied the knot after graduating. Peter and Sandra remain happily married with a son. Doug and Bev have a daughter but shortly after her birth, Bev catches Doug in bed with a man. Doug has subsequently moved to California, where Secter was living at the time, and entered into a long-term gay relationship. The film opens with a memorial for his deceased lover, who has presumably died of AIDS. Doug hasn't seen his daughter in two decades, but she surprises him by attending the service. She persuades him to return to Toronto for a class reunion, where he meets Peter, Sandra, and Bev. As the film was never shot (or even fully written) it's impossible to know how the script would have played out. But Secter's conception of the story provides some insight on how the characters' respective journeys in *Winter* might be read. According to this larger world, the climax of the film is a moment of self-discovery for Doug, where he comes to understand his feelings for Peter as attraction. But it's only several years later, with the breakdown of his marriage, that he's arrives at a point of self-acceptance and comes out as gay. Peter, in contrast, seems to be happily married to a woman. Based on this, it would appear that Doug's attraction to Peter is indeed primarily, if not exclusively, one-sided.

The Final Product

When compared with Secter's initial ambitions, the story of *Winter*'s production and release can seem like a long series of failures: the many technical challenges, the inability to secure funding, and the lack of commercial distribution among them. In actuality, it's a tale of almost unbelievable success. Going from initial inspiration to finished feature film in less than a year and producing something that screens at world-class festivals is a feat very few filmmakers, especially neophytes, achieve.

Secter's aspirations were obviously naive. But that naivety was pivotal in making the film a reality. Had he or anyone else on the team understood the sheer impossibility of what lay before them, they might never have tried it at all. The rush to start shooting meant working without a script. This in turn required the actors to develop much of their own dialogue, making the performances more natural, meaning that most scenes only needed one take. The result was a work that didn't look or feel like commercial films in the 1960s. And so *Winter* gained traction in art house and experimental settings, a shift that sometimes occurs with emerging artists who anticipate their work being viewed in one context only to find it has greater opportunities in another.

The goal had been to make a commercially viable independent film. It's a goal he arguably achieved, just not in the ways he had thought he would. He never secured commercial backing, but his skills as a negotiator and the good will of his creditors meant he was able to make the film without support. The failure to find a distributor, at least initially, served him well. By self-distributing, he both covered the costs of production and generated seed money for his next project, something most feature films, even big budget commercial endeavours, often fail to do.

Despite his early assertions of cinematic grandiosity, Secter's main goal was simply to produce a film of sufficient quality that it might be shown in theatres at home and abroad. Instead, he ended up being an unintentional trailblazer, as Matthew Hays writes, "working in the wilderness ... in a country that didn't have an industry to speak of, on a topic that hadn't really even been named" (Hays 2011). The arc of Secter's journey confirms a truism well known to anyone working with emerging creators: when artists don't understand the rules, they often break them in very interesting ways.

Chapter 4

What *Winter* Achieves

For me, high school was synonymous with isolation. As a queer kid who'd been a target of harassment since the age of five, I spent my teen years longing to escape the suburbs, dreaming of the freedom the city would bring. Six weeks after my eighteenth birthday, I finally arrived at university and a new kind of longing set in. Until then, my sexuality was something to be hidden. But living in a queer-positive residence meant that curious glances, subtle touches, and burgeoning friendships all became potential signs of romance. Interactions with my male peers were perpetually confusing. Situations were hard to read. Fearing rejection, I often found myself unable to make the first move and a different form of isolation began. Somehow, everyone but me understood the rules.

Following a long series of romantic rejections, I developed a crush on a guy in my theatre class. I'd assumed he was straight until, on one particularly drunken evening, we fooled around. After a handful of late-night dalliances, he struck up a flirtation with a girl in our year and the brief affair came to a halt. Livid, I assumed that she'd torn him away from me. It was years before I understood that his forays into bisexuality were mostly prompted by vodka shots and surging testosterone. I've since discovered that my story is not only common among my peers, it's arguably a rite of passage. Despite certain differences, Secter's film maps with surprising accuracy onto my own life.

The Critical Reception

In contrast to the relative scarcity of contemporary scholarship, *Winter* received an initial flurry of critical attention. This seems to have less to do with it being seen as a grand cinematic achievement than with the novelty of a student movie making it to Cannes. Major outlets including the *New York Times* and *Variety* covered it, along with the influential film magazines *Sight and Sound* and *Cahiers du cinéma*. Responses varied widely. Kevin Thomas of the *Los Angeles Times* lauded it, saying, "At a time when psychedelic effects and *cinéma-vérité* are fashionable with young film-makers it is reassuring to find one who is not only willing to tackle the hardest challenge of all, the traditional narrative form, but also to succeed so well with it" (Thomas 1968). Perhaps sporting some hometown pride, the *Winnipeg Tribune*'s Heather Robertson was even more effusive, closing her review with the line, "it is a work of art and one of the most appealing films I have ever seen – and intend to see again" (Robertson 1966). The worst notice was probably Gene Youngblood at the *Los Angeles Free Press*, who called it "incredibly naive, crude and uninteresting," adding that it "belongs to the New Cinema only because it was independently made for less than $8000. In no other sense could it be considered 'new', and only loosely could it be categorized as cinema" (Youngblood 1968).

Many reviews pointed to the issues with sound. *Variety* suggested that this weak spot, when paired with "stilted dialogue," made *Winter* better suited for university film societies than for commercial release (*Variety* 1966). The *New York Post*'s Frances Herridge called the audio "unfortunate," noting that viewers had to strain to hear the "inadequate sound track" (Herridge 1968). Writing for *Take One*, fledgling film critic and future A-list producer Joe Medjuck flagged the same problems along with the "sometimes crude" editing, but still called the film "engrossing and entertaining" (Medjuck 1966).

Of the cinematography, *Variety* called the interior shots "stiff," while simultaneously praising the exterior scenes of Toronto at night and the university campus in winter (*Variety* 1966). *New York Times* critic Renata Adler dismissed the camera work as amateurish (albeit painstaking), but lauded the startling gloom of the dormitory locations, "with desks, beds and the shape of the rooms themselves so depressingly alike" (Adler 1968). This assessment was echoed by Thomas at the *Los Angeles Times*, who said, "the bleakness of existence … comes through with stinging sharpness" (Thomas 1968), as well as the *Village Voice*, which praised "the most indescribably depressing background of insentient college dormitory life ever to be realistically evoked in films" (Stoller 1968). Writing in 2002 for a screening of the film at the University of Toronto, student journalist Kate Wilczak noted that the rooms of Sir Daniel Wilson residence "appear to have remained unchanged since '65" (Wilczak 2002).

Responses to the acting were varied. Regarding Labow and Tarvainen's performances, Thomas declared them "virtually perfect" (Thomas 1968). *Variety* wrote, "David Secter has done his job with a ring of the truth but his effort is left with an awkward air" (*Variety* 1966). Medjuck called the acting "at times clumsy" (Medjuck 1966). Frank Morriss of the *Globe and Mail* labeled the dialogue "workman-like," adding that the team faltered when "dealing with sustained scenes that require the touch of professional actors and the shrewd hand of a seasoned director" (Morriss 1965). He did manage some subtle praise, saying, "Of the two main performances, Labow gives the best account of himself, but Tarvainen, after showing a lack of contrast in the first few scenes, grows in acting stature. Janet Amos, as the serious-minded girl, has charm, and Joy (Fielding), as the lady of light morals, has vivacity." Adler was more complimentary, saying, "Henry Tarvainen plays the introvert – intense, honest, almost cross-eyed with sweetness and sensitivity. John Labow is the older boy, combining casualness and love in a very difficult part. Joy (Fielding) and Janet Amos, who play their respective girls, are excellent" (Adler 1968). Robertson was enamoured, calling the performances "extraordinarily touching and adept" (Robertson 1966).

Of all the film's elements, the screenplay was arguably the most well-received. The *Village Voice* said that Secter "develops his characterizations with a humorous intelligence that can't have much precedent in fiction films so cheaply made" (Stoller 1968). Morriss applauded the film's narrative complexity, saying, "Secter has a story that is hard for amateurs to do" but as the film progresses it "begins to go down the drain, and lose direction," fumbling towards "an inconclusive finale" (Morriss 1965). Notably he also lamented the ambiguous ending of Owen's *Nobody Waved Good-bye* (Morriss 1964), a key influence for Secter, but praised the same trait in Truffaut's *The 400 Blows* (Morriss 1960), another of Secter's inspirations. Herridge declared the film had "more character perception, better plotting nuance and livelier dialogue than many Hollywood productions," but agreed that the story was "inconclusive" (Herridge 1968).

Morriss's take on the ending may be down to the fact that he only saw "overtones of homosexuality," a position shared by the London *Times*, which called it the story of "an ambiguously close campus friendship between two very different young men," sidestepping any direct mention of queerness (Dixon 1997, 143). Thomas caught this element but tiptoed around naming it, saying that Doug "observes his friend's progress with a growing jealousy that speaks of an emotional involvement he is afraid to face" (Thomas 1968). Other critics addressed it plainly. Richard Roud was clearly aware of the content, writing in *Sight and Sound* that "it is the womanizing older boy who falls desperately – and unrequitedly – in love with the younger one" (Roud 1966a). His review for the *Guardian* was even more direct; there he called it "an unfulfilled homosexual romance" (Roud 1966b). *Variety* noted "an appealing handling of a heavily implied but not activated homosexuality" that is "carefully treated" but "never verbalized" (*Variety* 1966). Medjuck questioned the relevance of the queer elements, saying, "they seem to have been put in to add some sort of 'drama' to a plot whose effectiveness lies in the fact that it is so undramatic" (Medjuck 1966).

One of the most detailed write-ups came from James Stoller at the *Village Voice*, a proofreader for the publication who briefly wrote the film column "16 mm." Together with Roger Greenspun, he also ran the short-lived but influential cinema journal *Moviegoer* from 1964–66 (not to be confused the mid-1980s celebrity-laden magazine of the same name). Early in his review, Stoller compared the film's aesthetic and narrative qualities to "those innocent grade school educational films on Making Friends," (Stoller 1968) offering an unintentional nod to film culture in *Winter*'s country of origin. Neither Secter nor composer Paul Hoffert had sought to mimic the NFB. But since both were steeped in the works of Canada's dominant producer, it's no surprise their film would unconsciously exude mid-century Canadianness. Stoller built on this later, saying, "Learning in the true sense, however, is Secter's subject, and the film that looks uncomfortably at times like something to be projected in a classroom turns out to be in fact an 'educational' film. The continuing, painful, and barely escapable interpersonal confusions of the residential college life are finally understood as valuable, even integral to the educative process."

It's a sentiment echoed by Secter in *The Best of Secter*: "I was totally ignorant," he says. "I thought the clapperboard was just to make a loud noise so that everybody knows you're going to start shooting and shuts up. I didn't realize it had another function to actually synch up the picture and the sound until the first day we started shooting ... Nobody involved had any experience doing any of this stuff before. The actors had mostly done some theatre. None of us had written a script before. We had all done a little bit of writing. One of the cameramen had actually used a movie camera before but that was it. So it was really a student film in the truest sense of the word. We were all learning as we went along" (Secter 2005).

Beyond its length, what made Stoller's review notable is its discussion of the film's queerness. He pointed out things only a gay viewer is likely to see, an odd turn given that he often covered queer films without examining or even acknowledging this element. His review of Warhol's *Bike Boy* (a motorcycle fetish film in the lineage of *Scorpio Rising*) made only passing reference to "homosexual clothiers" as supporting characters, ignoring the director's near-masturbatory objectification of his heterosexual male star (Stoller

1967a). And he completely sidestepped the subject's queerness in his review of Shirley Clarke's *Portrait of Jason*, a documentary about a drag queen slash sex worker (Stoller 1967b). But for some reason, he spilled considerable ink on this aspect of *Winter.* He's also the only critic I've found who compared Secter's work to fellow Canadian director Sidney J. Furie's more overtly queer film, *The Leather Boys*, specifically in reference to the endings. (In *Winter*, Doug is forced to confront his attraction to his friend, but the attraction is never vocalized. In *The Leather Boys*, the gay character's sexuality is revealed, pushing his friend away.)

Stoller also commented on two elements I've not seen addressed elsewhere: the cartons of homogenized (homo) milk that appear in the cafeteria scene and in Peter's room, and the many excuses "for the innocent freshman's enormous heavy ass to be practically shoved into the camera." In the case of the milk, the first time the "homo" pops up, it's barely visible, likely to be seen only by those actively hunting for gay references. On subsequent appearances, the cartons aren't even in focus, meaning the "homo" can only be inferred. (Secter claims he only clocked the gay dairy after it was pointed out in the review.) As for the "enormous heavy ass," this seems to be entirely a function of camera placement in the cramped shooting locations.

Stoller also made one of the stranger assertions about the story arc that I've come across, saying that Peter's inability to read Doug's interest justifies the final confrontation between them, when "our coveted innocent freshman can truly be understood to deserve the punishment he gets." This analysis fails to account for two things. The first is the power dynamic their age difference creates. When you're struggling to find your footing, you latch on to what's available. A confused eighteen-year-old away from home for the first time isn't likely to have the emotional intelligence or motivation to question the intentions of an affable twenty-something offering the companionship he desperately needs. Teenage responses are often less polluted by cynicism and suspicion than those of adults. Peter isn't leading anyone on; his interest in Doug is largely born of Doug's interest in him. The second way in which

Stoller's analysis falters is that it presumes Peter should be able to read Doug's interest as sexual attraction. It's not until the final moments of the film, when he's reading *The Waste Land*, that Doug begins to understand his true feelings for Peter. Why then should Peter, the younger of the pair, be responsible for recognizing Doug's interest in him when Doug can't see it for himself?

These blind spots aside, Stoller did address the moments of true physical chemistry that other critics either ignored or merely hinted at. The story, he wrote, "progresses toward confirmations of meaning so confidently understood that Secter can afford nearly to throw them away: the not-quite embraces of Doug and Peter in the shower room and in the snow, followed by quick discreet fade-outs which are both logical and funny – or sad – in that they could not possibly be taken as euphemisms for anything." He positioned Secter's embrace/fade-out editing formula as a way to ensure nothing greater is read into these moments, eliminating the presumption of a hookup post snow romp or shower flirtation.

The notion of "meaning so confidently understood" is tricky, because Stoller didn't clarify whom he is speaking about. Queer people? Other critics? The general public? He may have been saying the queer elements are so clear that it isn't necessary to be more direct. If so, he failed to grasp Secter's creative circumstances. Avant-garde directors in New York and San Francisco could include overt queer content, since they had the resources with which to make their films and venues that would screen them. In Secter's case, this same material would have led campus administrators to kibosh the project before a single frame was shot. Even if he'd managed to evade university censors, there simply wasn't a home in English Canada for work with explicit sexual content. (Case in point: With its depictions of heterosexual coupling, Larry Kent's *The Bitter Ash* failed to find commercial distribution and was largely banned [Pevere 2003].) Although Stoller opened his review with an unintentional nod to the NFB, he ultimately fails to fully understand the context in which *Winter* was made.

The clearest insights on how Secter's circumstances shaped the film's content don't come from mainstream journalists or industry publications. Instead, this aspect is best addressed by a student newspaper. *Varsity* writer Arthur Zeldin published more about *Winter* than anyone, making his articles among the most useful for understanding the film – in part because they're the most biased. Zeldin and Secter were friends, having worked together at the paper. He had a unique understanding of the work's trajectory; he'd supported the project by writing about it throughout the creative process and even had a small role in it, appearing in the dinner party scene as a friend of Doug and Bev's (Zeldin 1965b). As a result, he's perhaps the only critic who can accurately address the film as a product of its time and place.

Frequently acting as a Secter booster, Zeldin penned an announcement about the film starting production that included the fawning conclusion, "Says Secter about the prospects of the picture: 'I think that our film will rank with any other Canadian feature yet made.' If the astounding success of the last two weeks is any clue, he just might do it" (Zeldin 1964). His other early articles included a desperate pitch for extras (Zeldin 1965c), the notice of Secter forming his company Varsity Productions (Zeldin 1965a), and a piece praising *Winter* (at that point only partially shot) as more worthy of discussion than the upcoming Academy Awards, where big budget musicals *My Fair Lady* and *Mary Poppins* reigned supreme (Zeldin 1965b). In his final piece, and based only on having seen rushes, he called the script, acting, and technical accomplishment "impressive" adding that "muk-a-muks of the professional film world … have expressed interest … even financial interest" (Zeldin 1965b; as best I can tell, the assertion of interest from "muk-a-muks," financial or otherwise, is a fabrication). These articles are clearly puff pieces but they point to something key in analyzing the film. *Winter* didn't emerge from a professional studio or an established independent art scene. Instead, it was the product of a community of people, including a budding critic named Arthur Zeldin who would go on to write for *Maclean's* and the *Toronto Star*.

Zeldin's longest text and only actual review of *Winter* opened with a statement that addresses the context in a way few critics, even the Canadian ones, managed to do. He notes that given the near-nonexistence of Anglo-Canadian film production, every homegrown film (including *Winter*) should be seen as significant, regardless of quality. He also recognized what a tremendous undertaking filmmaking is, saying, "It can easily be imagined how, at various points throughout the year-long production schedule, most everything possible went wrong at least once, most every hope petered out" (Zeldin 1965d).

In contrast to his earlier assertions about the film's impressive qualities (again, based on rushes), his take on the final product was often lukewarm: the dialogue is "marred by its excessive simplicity" and many of the scenes are "unremarkable, and perhaps even trite." Instead, Zeldin heaped considerable praise on Secter for his skill at grabbing attention, tracing a direct relationship between the filmmaker's many media appearances and the project's ultimate success. Applauding an artist's gift for self-promotion is often a backhanded compliment, if not an outright slag. But here, Zeldin seemed to be offering genuine praise, making the case that Secter would secure his own future stardom through his ability to occupy the spotlight.

What might be considered Zeldin's most insightful commentary is something no other critic could have offered. Having previously seen each of the film's leads in campus productions, he was able to situate their onscreen work in a longer series of roles. He remarked that Fielding was known for performances that "rely excessively on an appealing personality and a sexy presence" but that her turn in *Winter* showed "considerable authority and naturalness" despite "moments when her breathy beginnings detract from what she has to do." Amos's "richly-honed theatrical skills" sometimes let her down on screen, though she ultimately offers up "a very effective character." He complimented Tarvainen's acting chops and his "quiet intensity … with only an infrequent resort to mannerism." Of Labow, he said that he "has some false moments in the early part of the film" but ultimately "creates a brooding presence on screen which is quite forceful, and which, without much dialogue, fully articulates the emotional predicament his character arrives at."

The context of production (and the one in which he's writing his review) also come through in Zeldin's handling of the film's queer elements. He only hinted at the storyline, saying, "the end of the film sees Doug in an emotional crisis brought on by a totally new experience" and nodded to "the emotional predicament his character arrives at." Like the cast and crew, Zeldin understood that "gay" wasn't a word you said, and that accusations of homosexuality, even in a film review, could have dire consequences.

Although critical reception wasn't unanimously positive, one of the most common themes was that the film showed promise, both for Secter and the Canadian film industry. *Cahiers du cinéma*'s Louis Marcorelles called it "a first scribble, a simple notebook, but under the already demanding gaze of a real artist" (Marcorelles 1966; my translation). Writing in the *Toronto Star*, Robert Fulford said the film was "an interesting though uneven exercise," but as a student production, it was "an encouraging sign for all those people who are eagerly awaiting the birth of a Canadian film industry" (Fulford 1965). Herridge dubbed it "an amateur movie that should be the envy of many professionals" adding that, if Secter were given "some real money to work with good equipment he should do wonders" (Herridge 1968). Morriss declared that "Secter has the promise of doing some fine things … and when he masters this fully he might easily be a force on the Canadian film scene" (Morriss 1965). In the *Toronto Telegram*, Gerald Pratley suggested that the film showed great promise, which would be wasted unless he was "encouraged and given further opportunities" (Pratley 1965), an ironic statement considering Secter's future path.

Analyzing *Winter*

The second shot in *Winter* is an upward tilt that comes to rest on the word "UNION." These letters, seeming to float against the limestone columns of the city's main rail station, immediately situate the film in Toronto. The word also points to the movie's central plot: two people seeking connection who ultimately end up veering away from each other like trains headed for different destinations.

As the reviews indicated, *Winter* had numerous technical flaws. Secter had never worked with sync sound and no one on the volunteer crew knew anything about microphone placement. The problems with over- and underexposure (notably in the dining hall scene and certain evening shots) are common novice errors. The choppy editing reflects the struggle to produce a cohesive story based on usable footage. All of this is a natural part of an artist's evolutionary process.

Among critics, the acting was one of the more contentious issues. Responses ranged from high praise to outright pans. The performances aren't always good, but they're consistently brave. The film captures actors throwing themselves into an unfamiliar task: the occasional on-screen awkwardness serves as both a symbolic and a literal representation of the confusion and fear felt by Secter and his cast. As Jean-Luc Godard famously observed, narrative film is always a documentary about the actors making it, an idea furthered by Jacques Rivette, who saw every movie as a record of its own production and a window into the context that produced it (Lim 2010).

Every filmmaker has to face the gap between the work they conceive and the work they ultimately produce, a distance that's often more pronounced with younger artists, as they've yet to develop the skills to render their ideas in the way they'd hoped. We know from advance press that Secter aimed to make a film that would match both the commercial viability and the cultural cachet of the works that influenced him. If he'd had the knowledge, budget, and team to make a more polished work, he might well have reached that goal. Instead, his limitations led to something more in line with the field of art house cinema.

With this in mind, I propose that viewers embrace the film's unpolished elements as features that enhance the experience of the work, rather than dismissing them as rookie mistakes that need to be overlooked. The sound and image problems reveal the challenges the team experienced as they took their first steps into filmmaking, mirroring the uncertainty of coming out. The uneven editing, while not as sophisticated as the techniques characterizing the French New Wave, serves indirectly to capture the messiness of the characters' experiences, particularly in the opening section of Peter's arrival to the city. As Matthew Hays notes, from a contemporary perspective, this combination of elements can produce a certain nostalgia, "A deeply melancholic feeling … one that makes us long for the era in which such films were made" (Hays 2005b). These technical elements also frequently create a distancing effect, reminding us that we're watching a film – a common technique in experimental cinema during this time. With those works, the alienation is intentional. In Secter's case it's a byproduct of inexperience, but the effect is the same. While *Winter* isn't an experimental film per se, it *was* a grand experiment for the people who made it.

Toronto: The City as Character

In both contemporaneous reviews and current criticism, *Winter* is often dubbed a "Canadian" film for its site of production and the geography it portrays, which are overtly identified through recognizable locations and cultural references (Davidescu 2008). Even its name, as Matthew Hays notes, "could very well be the quintessential Canadian movie title" (Hays 2011). While technically accurate, the label is arguably insufficient. During this period, it's difficult to speak of "Canadian" film. Instead of a national cinema, there are three distinct strands segregated by language and geography emerging in Montreal,

Toronto, and Vancouver. It's therefore more accurate to speak of *Winter* not as a Canadian film but as a *Toronto* film, and to consider it within a lineage of films made in and about the city.

As former Toronto International Film Festival executive director Piers Handling notes, "Toronto did not effectively exist on film as either a physical site or an imaginative space for the first half century of the history of cinema" (Handling 2009, 15). However, *Winter* is one of a handful of fiction films, along with Don Owen's *Nobody Waved Good-bye* and Don Shebib's *Goin' Down the Road*, that put the city on screen. Secter's choice to unabashedly highlight his daily stomping ground is partly a product of his influences. The directors who inspired him (notably those of the French New Wave and Italian Neorealism) often did the same, ditching the sterility of the studio for the commotion of the streets. This is the moment when the concept of the city-as-character alongside the principal actors really begins to blossom: Rome is cast as a bustling metropolis of sensuality and corruption, Paris an unforgiving locale where dreams are dashed as easily as they're born, London a hotbed of swinging decadence, and (some years later) New York as the third character in Big Apple love triangles.

Toronto's cinematic CV is unusual in this regard. Far more often, it serves as a character actor in a supporting role rather than a flamboyant and easily identifiable lead, its visual banality making it a kind of chameleon (Handling 2009, 15). The lack of distinguishing features has made it an effective stand-in for Chicago, Pittsburgh, New York, and in the case of *The Handmaid's Tale* TV series, the dystopian theocracy of Gilead. Secter, Owen, and Shebib's works are therefore unusual within the broader history of Toronto-made cinema in that they make no attempt to hide their location. They were among the first to prove that Toronto is not only capable of standing in for other places but can also perform different versions of itself. With *Nobody Waved Good-bye*, the city is a wasteland for disaffected youth. In *Goin' Down the Road*, it's a soul-crushing desert masquerading as a beacon of possibility. From this perspective, *Winter* is remarkable for its positive view of Toronto, a clear reflection of Secter's relationship with his new hometown. Unlike Owen and Shebib's works, which conclude with the protagonists fleeing the city, *Winter* is a story of arrivals (Hays 2009, 139). As a new transplant, Secter met Toronto with wide-eyed wonder, taking in everything it had to offer intellectually, culturally, and sexually – an experience mirrored in Peter when *Winter* began shooting two years later. The film isn't just set *in* Toronto; it's also very much *about* Toronto, portraying it as a place of youthful possibility, devoid of the cynicism and alienation we see in works by Don McKellar and David Cronenberg decades later.

The bulk of *Winter* takes place at the University of Toronto. A frequent shooting location with the same shape-shifting quality as the rest of the city, it's served as a backdrop for numerous Hollywood blockbusters, including *Good Will Hunting* (1997), *Mean Girls* (2004), *The Incredible Hulk* (2008), and *Crimson Peak* (2015), as well as the low-budget slasher classic *Black Christmas* (1974). Secter renders the campus with considerable affection: the sprawling green spaces, the quirky mix of Victorian, Neo-Gothic, and Brutalist architecture, the formality of the dining halls, the claustrophobia of the dorms, the wild abandon of the parties. His portrayal reflects his own position: having been there only two years, he was no longer naive but not yet jaded. His take is joyful but realistic, a vision of student life that could only be created by someone currently living it.

The film's other key location is Yonge Street, the arterial road dividing the city into east and west. It's where Doug and Peter take an evening stroll past neon signs, dive bars, and burlesque joints. The Strip, as it was colloquially known, also features prominently in *Nobody Waved Good-bye* (where the film's lead goes to shoplift) and *Goin' Down the Road* (where the main characters hit on women and shop for records). As Geoff Pevere notes, this section of Yonge symbolized Toronto's bustling urbanity, a counterpoint to more dignified local landmarks such as Queen's Park or Nathan Phillips Square (Pevere

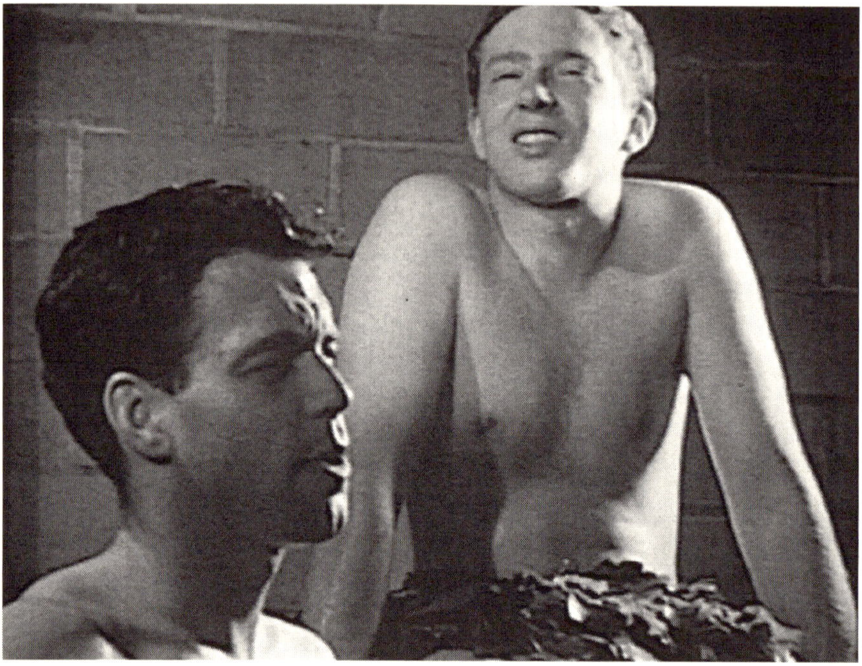

Figure 26
"How come I never see you around with any of the regular crowd?" "Oh, I don't know. Maybe I just like to take my time choosing my friends."

2009, 41). Like the early shots of the city, we view the Strip through Peter's eyes as he gleefully absorbs this new world of possibility, far from his sedate life in small-town Northern Ontario.

Doug and Peter don't visit any gay bars on their night out. But their frolicking happens not far from the city's blossoming gay quarter, an area Secter was known to frequent; Club 511, the Famous Door, the St Charles Tavern, and the Roman Baths were just blocks away (McLeod 1996, 281–2). Their visit to the Strip, an area where straight sexuality was prominently on display, becomes inadvertently symbolic of their unknowing proximity to queerness. (Notably, their evening ends in a Finnish sauna; Doug has shared his urban culture with Peter and Peter offers one of his own traditions in return.)

The Toronto that Secter portrays isn't one I ever experienced. I have fuzzy childhood memories of flashing neon signs on Yonge from the odd time we drove through the area at night. By the time I was a teenager, able to grab a bus downtown with friends, the Strip (where we'd shop for imported CD singles and dubious-looking fake IDs) had been largely revamped. Today, nearly every block has been demolished and rebuilt; seedy bars and arcades have been replaced by glossy brand-name retailers and bland fast-food joints, although the legendary Zanzibar strip club (which features in *Winter*) lives on. The views we see of the Lakeshore during Doug's arrival have been similarly altered, with colonies of glass condo towers dividing the city from the water.

Even though these scenes represent a version of the city I never witnessed first-hand, I still get a charge from seeing them; perhaps this is how Secter felt when he saw *Nobody Waved Good-bye*, and what David Cronenberg experienced when he saw *Winter*, the film he credits with catalyzing his journey into filmmaking. "In Toronto at that time, movies were not made," he says. "They came from somewhere else, just like automobiles came from somewhere else … I remember being absolutely astonished to see a movie that had my friends in it as actors and that had locations that I walked by every day at the University of Toronto. That was an incredibly shattering revelation for me" (Secter 2005). The feeling I have is different from what Secter and Cronenberg experienced in one important way. The version of Toronto they saw on film was the same city they experienced daily. But when I watch *Winter*, I know I'm seeing a version of the city that's gone, reminding me of the rapid pace of change.

Queering the Creative Process (Or Not)

The question of how to define queerness has long been a thorny subject. Numerous theorists including Lee Edelman, Annamarie Jagose, and Eve Kosofsky Sedgwick, have suggested that the term "queer" is both indefinable in its boundaries and contentious in its application (Edelman 2004, 17; Jagose 1996, 1; Sedgwick 1993, 8–98). Anthropologist Max Kirsch offers a starting point with his discussion of the emergence of queer theory as a discipline, stating that gay and lesbian studies are a subject matter, while queer theory is an *approach* to that subject matter (Kirsch 2006, 25). If Kirsch's idea of subject matter versus approach is extended to filmmaking, we could say that gay and lesbian films (as well bi and trans films) are works that address these subjects, whereas queer film is an approach to addressing these subjects.

Writer David J. Getsy identifies queerness as a "relational practice," stating that whether it's in the context of a romantic relationship or a "hostile society" opposed to expressions of difference, "one cannot be queer alone" (Getsy 2017, 254). Extrapolated to filmmaking, we may then say that queer filmmaking is a practice which operates relative to other queer people and in opposition to Getsy's "hostile society." As Gregg Bordowitz says, "A particular work is queer if it is viewed as queer, either by queers or bigots" (Bordowitz 1993, 211). As Richard Dyer points out, queer film emerges from the tradition of underground cinema, which provided space for gays and lesbians to represent themselves in ways that mainstream film would not (Dyer 2003, 110). A queer filmmaking approach may then be one that operates from a marginal position, an idea supported by Bordowitz, who ties queer art production to a "limited amount of resources" (Bordowitz 1993, 212).

There's also the sticky terminological question of "gay" versus "queer." Film writing often places considerable emphasis on situating works (and writers) in one of these two camps. But as Brett Farmer notes, there is both a challenge in precisely delineating these terms and a value in keeping their boundaries blurry. In the introduction to *Spectacular Passions: Cinema, Fantasy, Gay Male Spectatorships*, he says that he often uses the terms interchangeably in order to "replicate the sense of definitional heterogeneity … vital for a reasoned analysis of gay subjectivities and/or spectatorships" as well as a way to "avoid any oversimplified stabilization of these terms" (Farmer 2000, 15).

Working from Kirsch's idea of queerness as an approach, Getsy's concept of queerness as relational, and Dyer's point about queer film having its origins in the underground, I want to begin by considering queer film from the standpoint of how it is made. Frequently lacking access to the same opportunities as their heterosexual counterparts, queer filmmakers have often used a distinctive approach to creation: a "queer process," or perhaps a "queering of process."[1]

The first element of this approach is attitudinal. Queer artists typically lacked the resources and training to make work that would be accepted by the dominant culture. At the same time, they usually didn't bother fighting for space in a world that actively rejected them. They didn't need to because they had an existing community that wanted to hear their stories. Instead of waiting for permission from a gatekeeper, they just found a camera and made their work. From this perspective, *Winter* is an interesting case. Secter went into the process with almost no experience, figuring it out as he went along. However, his attitudinal approach stands in contrast to contemporaneous queer filmmakers in that he was intent on making a film with mainstream cachet. He wasn't aiming to speak to the queer community because he wasn't really part of it.

This leads to the second element: a focus on collaboration. Lacking resources, queer filmmakers have frequently relied on volunteer crew and performers from within their social circles, a process intrinsically tied to the experience of queerness – you come out, you find your people, you make art together. Many queer films might therefore be more accurately described as the product of communities rather than of individual directors (notably John Waters's *Dreamlanders* and Andy Warhol's *Factory Superstars*). Secter's situation was different; he was clear from the beginning that *Winter* was *his* film. Yes, nearly every aspect was highly collaborative, from the conception of the characters to the creation of the script to the editing. But unlike many directors who work with an existing group, Secter had to create the team that would make the film. The community he assembled wasn't queer. Most of them didn't even know he was gay. It was also temporary, largely dissolving with the end of the project. On this level, Secter had less in common with his contemporaries than filmmakers of previous generations like Nicholas Ray and Vincente Minnelli, who created works subtly addressing queer identity, with the production team largely in the dark about their director's sexuality.

The third element of queer process relates to the technology used. Lacking big budgets and specialized training, queer filmmakers have often turned to the most accessible media. Since it emerged in the mid-1960s, Super 8 has been hugely popular; Andy Warhol, Kenneth Anger, and Jack Smith all used it then, as did John Waters, Derek Jarman, and David Wojnarowicz a generation later, and G.B. Jones and Bruce LaBruce a generation after that. Despite being supplanted by more accessible media, the format has seen continued use among queer filmmakers today including Kika Thorne, Scott Fitzpatrick, Allyson Mitchell, and the duo Shawna Dempsey and Lori Millan.[2] In the 1980s consumer-grade video offered a similar boost to Keith Haring and Nelson Sullivan, and years later to archival projects like Jonathan Caouette's *Tarnation* (2003) and Jim Hubbard's *United in Anger: A History of ACT UP* (2012). Geared to the general public, both Super 8 and VHS allowed the capture of images at relatively low cost and without specialized knowledge. More recently, directors have been using smartphone cameras to tell queer stories, including straight filmmaker Sean Baker's *Tangerine* (2015; about a pair of trans sex workers) and the many short films commissioned as part of "In Your Pocket," a long-running series for Toronto's Inside Out LGBT Film Festival that I co-curated with Marcin Wisniewski through our platform, RT Collective. In Secter's case, he wanted to shoot on 16 mm but didn't have the budget to buy film. Instead, he used short ends and opted for black and white over colour to make transitions between film stocks less noticeable. He used mostly professional grade gear, though it was largely borrowed, sometimes surreptitiously. He didn't insert Super 8 sequences as a cost-saving measure, a favourite technique of Waters. He did, however, borrow a collection of stills from *The Varsity* to create the early campus-life montage. As with other aspects of the process, his approach was less a deliberate choice than a product of circumstances.

Of course, none of these elements are the exclusive property of queer artists. Many marginalized creators (especially racialized and feminist filmmakers) have employed similar strategies. Different parts of the queer community also face different barriers, so while the elements I have laid out can be broadly applied to queer filmmaking, they are neither universal nor exhaustive. However, these elements point to artists operating outside the mainstream who, for the most part, revel in that position.

Saunas, Showers, and Snowfalls: Unpacking *Winter*'s Queerness

The first aspect I want to address when discussing the film's content is the way Secter deals with space. The all-male dormitory, the sauna, and the locker room are immediately recognizable to gay viewers as sites where desire is awakened (coming out), remembered (masturbation), and enacted (bed-hopping in the dormitory, cruising and voyeurism in the other two). At the same time, due to homophobic harassment and violence, they are often environments where fear and arousal are intermingled, as evidenced by the massive volume of gay porn centred on locker room and dormitory hazing rituals. Through their placement in the film, Secter consciously used these locations to forward the gay storyline. To queer viewers, they situate the film as a narrative of sexual awakening.

Another key site in this regard is the setting for the critical snow scene. Many writings incorrectly describe this part in the film as a "snowball fight." Instead, Doug and Peter, seeing the quad covered with pristine powder, decide to run across it haphazardly in shirtsleeves, asserting their presence within the university by inscribing their bodies on the space through their footprints. Rather than occurring in a space already known as a site of queer sexual

Figure 27
The cast doff their clothes and prepare to hit the showers.

attraction, we may interpret this as a means of etching queer desire onto an aggressively heterosexual environment, a "queering of space." This scene also seems to be a key turning point in Doug's attraction. Later, during the walk to the library, he and Peter discuss it:

> Doug: Remember that first snowfall?
> Peter: How could I forget it? It was my first hangover. I don't think I've been quite the same since.
> Doug: No, neither have I.
> Peter: You? Yeah, I guess you have changed.

Here, both seem to be subtly acknowledging a shift in Doug's feelings brought on by the experience. At the same time as they queer the space, the action seems to stimulate queer sexual arousal, in one of them at least.

Queering extends to cultural objects, where traditionally straight works receive a queer spin. We see a version of this when Doug sings the song "Tuoll on mun kultani (Far Away Is My Love)," for Peter. Notably, he performs this while sitting next to Bev, his girlfriend. The true object of his interest isn't the

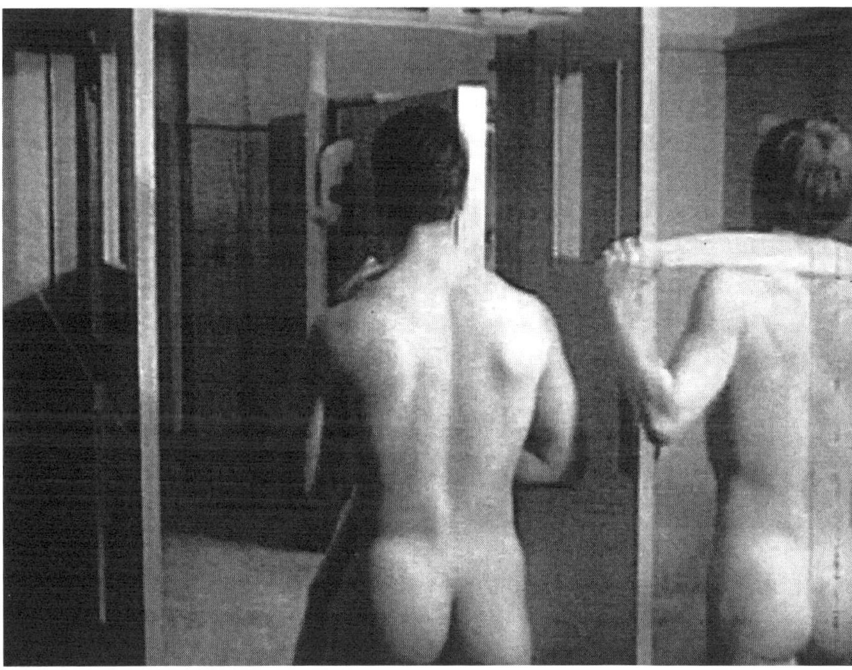

Figure 28
"The actors were all very comfortable with the nudity," Secter says. "At that point, men still swam nude at Hart House, so it wasn't strange for them to be naked together on set."

Figure 29
"Remember that first snowfall?"

person beside him but the one impossibly far away in terms of their ability to truly connect. Here, Secter takes a traditional and presumably heterosexual piece of art and reimagines it as an expression of queer sexuality. Originally, the song speaks of being separated from the person you love by geographic distance. In the film, it refers to being kept apart by social norms.

A subtler version of this happens with Secter's use of *The Waste Land* to bracket the film. During the first library scene, when Peter is borrowing Eliot's book, Doug comments, "I tried reading through this once. Couldn't make much sense of it." At the conclusion of the film, he returns to the library and

Figure 30
From *The Waste Land*: "April is the cruellest month, breeding / Lilacs out of the dead land, mixing / Memory and desire, stirring / Dull roots with spring rain."

rereads the first lines of the poem, which propel him to grasp his feelings for Peter. Eliot's poem becomes a metaphor for Doug's feelings; it suggests he previously experienced some measure of same-sex attraction though he "couldn't make much sense of it." Now, through his relationship with Peter, he has come to a realization about his sexuality.

A second aspect of queer content is the way desire is expressed through the eyes, a technique which, as Lauren Rohrs notes, has long been used as a way "to alert the audience of a character's sexual orientation without the need to revert to stereotypes, iconography, or exaggeration" (Rohrs 2019, 21). Much of the attraction in the film is expressed through moments when Doug looks at Peter. As mentioned, Secter didn't give Labow explicit direction to perform sexual interest, nor was it written into the script. Still, when Doug looks at Peter his yearning is obvious, particularly in contrast to the way he looks at Bev. Secter's success in getting an actor to unintentionally portray attraction may come down to a mix of casting and editing. Certain performers (and I would put Labow in this category) simply exude sex on screen; it's less of a conscious choice than something inherent in their manner. In Labow's case, his natural sensuality, in combination with holding glances at Peter just a little too long, turn what could have played as platonic interest into painful longing.

The third aspect relates to moments where Doug touches Peter: a casual pat on the back or a brush on the arm alternately appear to be a gesture of friendship or an expression of sexual interest, depending on the perspective of the viewer. Context is key in reading this element. As Secter explained to me, men in the 1960s actually had *more* freedom to touch each other; social doctrine prohibited the mention of homosexuality, even as a joke, so casual contact wasn't interpreted as an indicator of sexual attraction. There are also key moments which suggest the interest is one-sided: the embrace after the snow scene, the attempted hug post-winter break, and the moment backstage when Doug spontaneously plants a kiss on Peter's cheek. In each case, Doug is the initiator and Peter rejects him: pushing him away (the snow scene), avoiding his touch (after the winter break), or simply ignoring him (the kiss). Perhaps the queerest of these moments is actually one of violence – the climax of the film when Doug knees Peter in the groin after learning he has had sex with Sandra, an act typically celebrated with a handshake or a pat on the back. Decidedly out of character with Doug's ultra-masculine posturing in the rest of the film, it's also a dually feminizing (and therefore arguably queer) gesture. By hitting below the belt, Doug symbolically castrates Peter at the same time as he emasculates himself (a form of metaphorical self-castration) by breaking a fundamental tenet of manliness, representing a pivotal moment in understanding his sexuality and the corresponding crisis in his masculinity.

Winter's Lineage and its Disappearance

As far as 1960s Anglo-Canadian films go, *Winter*'s disappearance is not unusual. Most of the artists and many of the works from this decade have faded from our broader cultural consciousness. Directors who achieved mainstream recognition (including Norman Jewison, Sidney J. Furie, and Arthur Hiller) mostly departed for the US or the UK, since international gatekeepers were largely uninterested in Anglo-Canadian film. With few exceptions, the directors who did continue to produce work did so in obscurity. As Matthew Hays told me, "Many of those filmmakers suffered terribly. They were brave, they were audacious, and they made these films in a figurative wilderness without the backing of the feature film industry. And then there was no one there to support them. No funding. No community. There was nothing. So a lot of them floundered. For most, there was no way to keep going" (Matthew Hays, interview with author, 9 December 2020).

Within mid-century Canadian cinema, *Winter* often gets ignored, which is odd given its prominence at the time of release. If the film is referenced in publications at all, it's usually, as Secter said, in the form of a footnote. Published in 1977, the *Canadian Film Reader*, one of the industry's foundational texts, fails to even mention it. Thomas Waugh attributes this exclusion to passive heterocentrism, if not outright homophobia on the part of his fellow critics, adding "It really wasn't until the 1990s that incorporating 'queer' into national film histories became fashionable for non-queer historians and critics" (Thomas Waugh, interview with author, 11 December 2020). At the same time, it's also largely absent from books on queer film history. There's no trace of it in Darwin Porter and Danforth Prince's expansive volume *50 Years of Queer Cinema*, although the book does feature numerous Canadian entries, including *Outrageous!*, *The Fox*, *Fortune and Men's Eyes*, and *Leaving Metropolis*. It doesn't appear in either Parker Tyler's substantial work *Screening the Sexes* or Vito Russo's famed text *The Celluloid Closet*. It's even missing from 2017's *Any Other Way: How Toronto Got Queer*, a near-encyclopedic record of the city's LGBT history.

If *Winter* has been ignored within the field of Canadian cinema due to homophobia, why then has it also been largely forgotten within the field of queer film? The first possible reason for its exclusion is the way in which sexuality is represented in the work. As critic Radu Davidescu notes, the subtlety with which queerness is rendered "caused many (then and today) to doubt that it is a queer film at all" (Davidescu 2008). He goes on to say that the ambiguity with which the story is drawn mirrors the ambiguity experienced by both the characters and the viewer; they aren't really sure if they're gay and neither are we, a nod to the film's milieu where nascent homosexuality was likely to be greeted with denial.

In this regard, the film is part of an extensive body of work where gay identity is rendered in ways that make it invisible to straight people. The buddy film, which centres on a relationship between two male protagonists rather than a conventional male-female love story, is a key part of this history. This includes works like Howard Hawks's *Red River* (1948), featuring closeted actor Montgomery Clift, *Rebel Without a Cause* (1955), featuring openly bisexual star Sal Mineo and directed by the mostly closeted Nicholas Ray, and William Wellman's *Wings* (1927), a silent film about a romance between two World War I pilots, which features a brief nude scene and a gay kiss. Typically from different backgrounds and brought together by circumstance, the buddies often dislike each other initially but develop a rapport over time. Rather than serving as a romantic interest, female characters in the genre tend to hamper the relationship. As queer literary theorist Robert K. Martin notes, these stories are rooted in the mid-nineteenth century, a time when the status of male friendship was disrupted by the greater inclusion of women in what had historically been all-male spaces (Martin 1990, 169–70).

For some critics and theorists, the debate isn't around *Winter* being a queer film. Instead, it centres on whether it's queer *enough*. As Hays told me: "It's not as in-your-face as people might like. It's a very tender, subtle film that ends with a kind of surrender. From the perspective of more contemporary viewers, they might just not find it exciting enough. There's also the question of the film presenting a character not yet ready to fight for acceptance because they're still conflicted about their own sexuality, as opposed to an inspiring story of someone who knows who they are and is battling the forces of oppression" (Hays, interview). Waugh expands on this, saying: "There is a positive image dogmatism in gay film criticism that was very prevalent in the seventies and eighties, and still continues to some extent today. A certain kind of story is favoured and younger people watching films from that era may respond to them without any kind of sensitivity to what that historical period was like. At the same time, it's so important for a film like this to be preserved because it really speaks to what it was like to be gay in this time and place. It's a way to pass that on to future generations who have no other way to access it" (Waugh, interview). Far from failing to meet some imagined standard of sex radicalism established by artists like Anger, Smith, and Warhol, *Winter* points to the fact that explicit sexual representation is only one of the myriad ways in which queerness can manifest in filmmaking.

The subtlety with which the queer elements are rendered, in combination with the time in which *Winter* emerged, leads to a second possible reason for its disappearance: the historical position it occupies within the queer cinematic canon. *Winter* was produced at a time when outrageously explicit queer cinema was being made in the US. Yet Secter's film has more in common narratively with the works of earlier directors who told stories that would be palatable to straight people but resonate secretly with queer audiences. Nevertheless, the spirit of the film, from the way it was made to how it was distributed, is just as radical as much of the overtly queer work produced around that time. Occupying this liminal space, with one foot in the old and one in the new, may be part of the reason why the film "resists canonization" (Waugh 2001, 111).

The third possible reason for *Winter*'s disappearance is the question of distribution. Prominent gay and lesbian films have circulated through mainstream (presumably straight-owned and -operated) channels for some time. But the works that have secured distribution only make up a small fraction of those produced by queer artists and are largely restricted to titles considered likely to be profitable. Waugh also points to an obvious though often overlooked roadblock to preserving these histories – a lack of interest on the part of distributors when it came to archiving queer films. "It's true that technical issues were present, especially as 16 mm waned in the 1990s," Waugh says. "But that's also connected to filmmakers not taking the initiative to maintain their archives by investing in transfers to VHS and then later DVD. The inertia of the CFMDC [the Canadian Filmakers' Distribution Centre, the film's Canadian distributor] in not facilitating and encouraging this process is partly due to a certain lingering celluloid-centric narrow-mindedness. And there was also a weird default heterocentrism that assumed lesbian and gay identities couldn't possibly be marketing strategies" (Waugh, interview).[3]

In one way, the story of Secter's film is a story of disappearance: a work which marked a high point in Canadian cinematic history being nearly expunged from that same history a decade after it was made. At the same time, it can be read as a tale of dogged persistence. The reason it has clung to the edges of our cultural consciousness is that, as Secter points out, certain key people advocated for it. "If it weren't for Tom (Thomas Waugh), the film probably would have remained in obscurity. It largely disappeared in the 1970s, as there were no gay festivals at the time. Then, in the 1980s, he started writing about it and working to promote it. Thanks to him a new generation of moviegoers were able to see it, learn about it, and enjoy it. But if it wasn't for him, I don't think anyone would even know about it today, let alone be writing a book about it" (Secter, interview, 30 November 2020).

Given *Winter*'s technical flaws and uneven performances, few people would consider it an incredible achievement of cinema. But the film is unquestionably an incredible achievement in and of itself. The numerous challenges Secter faced with funding and production clearly illustrate the near impossibility of telling queer stories in 1960s Canada. Would the NFB have green-lit this film? Probably not, even if it had come from a more experienced director.[4]

From Secter's vantage point in the early 1960s, the idea that homosexuality would be decriminalized in Canada, let alone broadly accepted, was by no means assured. His drive to create the work had nothing to do with recording pre–Bill C-150 gay life for posterity. But the film still serves this purpose. Beyond that, *Winter* cements its position in the queer film canon by telling a story nearly every gay man can relate to – falling in love with your straight best friend.

Chapter 5

Memory and Desire

On 2 May 1915, at around 10 o'clock in the morning, a young man named Jean Jules Verdenal died on a battlefield on the Gallipoli peninsula of what is now Turkey. A medic for the French army during World War I, Verdenal perished instantly when a bullet from an enemy rifle pierced his forehead while he was administering first aid to a fellow officer. He was buried a short distance from the spot where he was killed, under the shade of a juniper tree not far from an olive grove (Perinot 2011, 43–4). As one of more than twenty million soldiers and civilians lost in the Great War, Verdenal could have easily faded from history. But two years later, his name appeared in the dedication for the first volume of poetry by an up-and-coming writer named Thomas Stearns Eliot.

For Jean Verdenal, 1889–1915
mort aux Dardanelles
la quantitate
Puote veder del amor che a te mi
  scalda,
Quando dismento nostra vanitate
Trattando Vombre come cosa salda

For Jean Verdenal, 1889–1915
Who died at Dardanelles
You may see
The measure of the love which
  warms me towards you
When I forget our insubstantiality
Treating shades as if they were solid
  and real
(Translation by John Peter)

Verdenal and Eliot met in 1910 while studying at the Sorbonne (Verdenal in medicine, Eliot in philosophy). They lived in the same rooming house in the Saint-Germain-des-Prés district of Paris until the summer of 1911, when Eliot left for Munich before ultimately returning to the US. Following their cohabitation, they exchanged a substantial volume of letters that recalled their time together with passionate intensity, suggesting something beyond ordinary friendship. The true nature of their bond has been the subject of considerable speculation ever since. In 1952, Canadian critic John Peter wrote "A New Interpretation of *The Waste Land*" for the magazine *Essays in Criticism* in which he suggested Eliot's revolutionary work was an elegy for a young male lover. Eliot subsequently threatened libel and insisted all remaining copies of the journal be destroyed. Peter republished the essay in 1969, four years after Eliot's death, including a post-script detailing the conflict and adding that the young man who inspired the poem was likely Verdenal.[1] His interpretation was echoed by both James E. Miller in *T.S. Eliot's Personal Waste Land* (1977) and Carole Seymour-Jones in *The Painted Shadow* (2001). According to Seymour-Jones, Eliot struggled with sexual inhibition throughout his life, a product of his intensely religious upbringing. Given this, she asserts that it's unclear whether his relationship with Verdenal ever became physical. But it was almost certainly romantic, even if the romance was ambiguous to both of them.

As an English major, Secter had a passing knowledge of Eliot's work. However, when he chose the title of his film, he knew nothing about the rumours surrounding Eliot's sexuality or the connection between *The Waste Land* and a possible gay romance. As Secter tells it, he simply felt the opening lines captured the fleeting nature of the connection he wanted to portray. His choice to reference a poem inspired by a sexually ambiguous relationship between two cohabitating male students five decades earlier could be entirely coincidental. It's also possible that he was drawn to something inherently queer in Eliot's work without even realizing it.

In my mid-teens, I developed a particular fascination with St Sebastian, which nearly resulted in a tattoo I'm now thankful I was too scared to get. (I settled instead for seven holes through my left ear, in a non-permanent tribute to his arrow-ridden body.) This was before I'd seen John Greyson's *Lilies* (1996) and Derek Jarman's *Sebastiane* (1976) or knew anything about the centuries-long homoerotic fixation with the perpetually suffering near-naked youth. It was only years later that I realized the sexualized paintings of his violent martyrdom, with their intermingling of persecution and desire, were references to the plight of homosexuals throughout history. Like Secter, I was drawn to queer art produced years before I was born without knowing it was queer. This ability to locate queer culture without a direct connection to other queer individuals has been a critical element in many people's coming-out processes and the broader formation of community.

Figure 31
The martyrdom of Saint Sebastian: Simon (Jason Cadieux) and Bilodeau (Matthew Ferguson) set up for their school play in John Greyson's *Lilies*.

Figure 32
Chock full of nudity and BDSM references, Derek Jarman's *Sebastiane* borders on softcore porn.

Most cultures, you're born into. But as a queer person, you enter the world an orphan, only seeking out your community once you've realized that you're part of it (Halperin 2012, 7). The de-prioritization of blood relationships in the shaping of queer life is part of the reason for the culture's emphasis on "chosen family," those bonds formed by choice rather than the accident of genetics or the sanction of the state. Because queer people were, and often continue to be, rejected by their families, these relationships can be a substitute for biological kinship (Weston 1997). Additionally, queer narratives within biological lineages are often hidden or destroyed – either by relatives in the hopes of concealing "shameful" histories or by queer people, who erase evidence of their own existence to keep themselves safe or shield their families from future embarrassment (Horvat 2021, 3–4). It's a practice referenced in *Victim*, Basil Dearden's 1961 film about a closeted gay lawyer, which concludes with the main character burning an incriminating photograph of himself with another man.[2]

In *Screening Queer Memory*, Anamarija Horvat emphasizes the place that cinema holds within this process. She argues that, in the queer community more than in other minority groups, memory is shaped by filmic representations and cinema can serve as a substitute for in-person contact with past generations,[3] something I see reflected in my own experience. Prior to having queer friends, much of my search for knowledge about my community happened at my local video store. The connections I found to historical figures aided my coming out process by showing me that I wasn't the only one going through the struggles I was experiencing.

The nature of queer culture has led to a specific set of practices associated with the preservation of memory. Oral histories have played a role, both those passed colloquially and formal initiatives like the ACT UP Oral History Project and the Lesbians Making History collective. But the historical transfer of memory in the gay community has been particularly dependent on art: painting, sculpture, poetry, and more recently photography, film, and digital media. Because queer identity has frequently been criminalized, artworks exploring these identities have often been rendered in ways that make them largely unreadable to the straight world. According to historian Bruce Bell, the lack of genetic relationship and the reliance on art have meant that the passage of queer memory often functions like a message in a bottle – a covert object tossed into the sea in the hopes it will one day be found and appreciated (Bruce Bell, interview with author, 15 April 2020).

These works of art may contain specific symbols or cultural references, making them uniquely recognizable to queer people. As Michael Bronski discusses extensively in the first chapter of *Culture Clash: The Making of Gay*

Sensibility, they are also formulated to help queer people recognize *themselves* by stimulating sexual desire (Bronski 1984, 23). The shower montage is certainly *Winter*'s most overtly homoerotic section, which Secter specifically included to forward the gay storyline. It's a scene that will cause gay viewers to both recall past sexual sparks associated with these spaces and to experience them in the moment. Here, Secter is tapping into a specific lineage of nudity and sexualized bodies in the history of gay art. With these works, the explicit depiction of sexual activity is unnecessary. The content is sufficient to trigger arousal, both in those who already understand their sexuality and those who are just beginning to: watching naked men on film won't make you gay, but the charge you experience in seeing them might help you realize that you are. Although these objects serve as vessels of queer history for future generations, they weren't always produced with this task in mind; the preservation and passage of memory is often a byproduct of their creation rather than a specific goal. Images of male couples on Roman pottery, erotic photographs by German artist Wilhelm von Gloeden, the poetry of Walt Whitman, and most of the body of work around AIDS were not created primarily as a record for future generations. But they still serve this purpose, much as *Winter* does with the time and place it documents.

The unique relationship queer people have with our shared past leads to another element in objects of queer memory: the combination of intentional and unintentional historical referentiality (Bronski 1984, 66). Gay physique magazines deliberately featured models mimicking poses from classical Greek statuary, early examples of queer sexuality encoded in art (Bronski 1984, 46).[4] Referentiality was particularly common in the New Queer Cinema movement of the early 1990s, where directors like Gregg Araki, Cheryl Dunye, Isaac Julien, and Gus Van Sant conspicuously wove visual references into their works including books, posters, and T-shirts on screen, music choices in the soundtrack, and allusions to other films in the dialogue. It's also something Secter did in a less overt way with *Winter*. During the scene when Bev confronts Doug about his relationship with Peter, we see a copy of Allen Ginsberg's *Howl*

(1956) strategically placed in the headboard shelf of his bed, a nod to one of the early 1960s' few openly gay writers. (According to Secter's telling, Peter has given this book to Doug as a gift, though this moment isn't shown on screen.) He also included two unintentional references to gay history: the lines from Eliot's poem used to bookend the film and Peter's reference to Shakespeare's *Richard II* in the bedroom scene.

As in other cultures where elders were taken from the community before their time and were therefore unable to share their stories, queer memory often requires an active search for history on the part of youth (Thomas 2011; Halperin 2012, 7). In addition to the other factors mentioned above, this aspect is shaped by the relationship queer culture has usually had with the wider society. While queer people have always existed, pockets of queer culture tend to emerge and dissipate in different locations at different points in time. The reasons for their emergence vary, but their dissolution is often the result of a shift in social values: the spread of Christianity through the Roman Empire, the rise of Nazism in 1930s Germany, post-war conservatism in the US. In all these cases, the destruction of gay culture is a conscious decision on the part of the ruling force. (The Reagan Administration's response to AIDS could also fit into this framework.) The loss of our elders means that, if we want to understand this history, we often have to do the work ourselves, reaching into the past to search for information rather than simply having it offered to us. This process requires the location, preservation, and dissemination of existing works – the survival of memory, after all, requires new acts of remembrance (Rigney 2016). Each shard of pottery, poem, and photograph that tells us something about queer history is here because someone chose to save it. In the case of *Winter*, I was able to discover the film because a tiny number of people actively worked to keep it alive in the cultural consciousness. And yet, in contrast with more prominent examples of gay historical narrative that I came upon in my high school library or local video store, I still had to go looking for it.

This already complex process of seeking out information is further impeded by generational conflict. In my late teens, I had numerous conversations with older people in which I was chastised, belittled, and dismissed for my lack of knowledge about queer history and queer culture in general. Rather than make me want to educate myself about my community's history, these interactions often had the opposite effect. Only years later did I come to fully comprehend how profoundly the generation that preceded mine was traumatized by AIDS – an experience that I, given my age, would never fully understand. As feminist writer Sara Ahmed says, "to be traumatized is to hold a history in a body" (Ahmed 2020). My elders carry a history within them and I have a responsibility to pass that history on. This realization taught me that I need to have a lot of patience, to persist in these conversations, and to enter them knowing I might never truly comprehend the experiences in question. These conversations with our elders are complicated because we are often speaking across lines of trauma and profound differences in lived experience. But we still need to have them.

Of course, none of the elements I've laid out above, including the importance of art and the conflict between generations, are exclusive to queer culture. Rather, it is their combination that sets queer memory apart. Additionally, while these traits are common to different strands of the broader queer community, searching for queer history is complicated by intersectional factors, including existing structural barriers and the lack of material representing certain identity groups. While I have been using the term "queer memory" for semantic simplicity, the concept functions better in the plural. Just as it is increasingly common to refer to a broader set of queer *communities* rather than a singular queer community, we may also think of a broad collection of queer *memories* rather than a universal "queer memory."

The process of writing this book has fundamentally been one of dialogue. Nearly all of these conversations were with queer elders, the people who've made it possible for me to enjoy the life of comparative freedom I've lived.

I've been fortunate to be able to collect information and insight from primary sources, including Secter and the surviving cast and crew, as well as film historians, critics, and activists. In order to understand *Winter*, I had to understand the context in which it was created. It was a time and place I thought I knew. But as I learned more about it, I came to realize how little I actually grasped. The brief mentions of Secter's work that I initially encountered barely scraped the surface of his efforts when it came to their complexity and historical significance. Many of the paths of discovery I followed began with random newspaper clippings, book dedications, and, in keeping with Secter's own words, footnotes. Now that I've pieced together the story of *Winter*, I'm left to wonder: What other critical moments of queer history have fallen through the cracks?

Notes

Chapter Two

1 The legislation decriminalized sex with two men in private. Groups larger than two, with men under the age of twenty-one, or in public spaces, still faced arrest. The act has long been seen as a turning point for gay rights. But as historian Tom Hooper notes in "Queering '69: The Recriminalization of Homosexuality in Canada," the impacts of Bill C-150 are questionable. While it demonstrated a growing public tolerance towards homosexuality, arrests of gay men cruising for public sex actually increased after its passage.

2 For a detailed look at the history of lesbian bars during this era, check out Lynne Fernie and Aerlyn Weissman's 1992 film *Forbidden Love: The Unashamed Stories of Lesbian Lives* and the corresponding book from the Queer Film Classics series by Jean Bruce and Gerda Cammaer.

3 Canadian films that have been the focus of books in the Queer Film Classics series include *À tout prendre* (Claude Jutra, 1963), *Il était une fois dans l'Est* (André Brassard and Michel Tremblay, 1974), *I've Heard the Mermaids Singing* (Patricia Rozema, 1987), *Zero Patience* (John Greyson, 1993), *Fire* (Deepa Mehta, 1996), and *C.R.A.Z.Y.* (Jean-Marc Vallée, 2005).

Chapter Three

1 The film premiered on 27 September 1965. A press release from the Commonwealth Film Festival archives proclaimed, "The much-discussed Canadian feature film – *Winter Kept Us Warm*, made by a group of students at the University of Toronto, gets its world premiere at Cardiff. Described by professional filmmakers in the U.S.A. and Canada as a very professional product of high technical and dramatic quality, *Winter Kept Us Warm* merits commercial distribution." Since the festival staff only saw the completed film for the first time at the screening, just as Secter did, their assertions about its quality, as well as the descriptions attributed to "professional filmmakers" appear to be a fabrication in line with Secter's own pattern of exaggerating professional interest in the film during production.

Chapter Four

1 As Noel Purdon writes, "what we understand by gay cinema cannot merely be the same as the depiction of gays in films. It includes the whole creative process and working relationship experienced by a gay mentality employed in the cinema" (Purdon 1976, 116).

2 In a 2013 interview, film programmer Scott Miller Berry told me, "I think of Super 8 as a queer format … It's not a pristine HD image. It's rough around the edges, soft focus. It's the low-budget underdog of film. It's also very beautiful and very accessible. Queers are very resourceful. We can just make shit happen. For me, Super 8 is tailor-made for that community. Its scarcity is both its drawback and its strength" (Dupuis 2013).

3 The CFMDC began cataloguing films with titles related to queerness in the 1980s (Human Sexuality in 1981, Homosexuality in 1984, and Gay and Lesbian in 1988). As queer works were not always easily identifiable

prior to this, there was an additional layer of challenge for programmers in finding them. *Winter* was not initially included under the "Homosexuality" label when it was introduced. The synopsis included no mention of sexuality; the relationship was described as a "close campus friendship" and an "unlikely attachment." It's difficult to know why this was the case, but there are two likely possibilities. Either the person cataloguing the films was unable to read *Winter* as queer or they were aware it was queer but felt that the film would have more screening opportunities if not labelled as such.

4 The NFB's first film to address queer sexuality was Susan Gabori and Janet Walczewski's *New Romance (Aspects of Sexuality and Sexual Roles)* released in 1975. A few additional films appeared in the 1980s, including Fernand Bélanger's *Passiflora* (1985), Moira Simpson's *Lorri: The Recovery Series* (1985), and Paul Crépeau's *Lettre à Tom* (1987).

Chapter Five

1 As Tim Dean notes, "Peter's essay reemerged in 1969 on the eve of Stonewall, the political rebellion that traditionally marks the birth of gay liberation. In retrospect, Peter appears to have brought Eliot out of the closet at exactly the historical moment that lesbians and gays throughout the United States became politically committed to mobilizing against the constraints that accompany enforced secrecy. There is a certain poetic justice in Eliot's being forced out of the closet along with everybody else" (Dean 2004, 51).

2 These practices are also enacted by the broader community. In "Disappearing the Queer," the epilogue to his memoir *All the Rage*, Canadian writer Brad Fraser discusses the historical habit of collective archival erasure. As Fraser notes, when a person who wasn't out to their family died, there was a communal practice where friends would go to their home in advance of family arriving to remove any hints of their sexual-

ity, allowing them to stay closeted in death, a practice that still happens today (Fraser 2021, 336).

3 Notably, the medium of cinema emerges around the same time as the concept of the homosexual as an identity. Perhaps a deeper connection exists between these two societal turning points.

4 In addition to connecting works with a longer trajectory of queer iconography, the choice to situate images in an imaginary historical time period also helped creators evade censorship. As Jeff Auer notes, beefcake magazines often employed motifs like gladiator costumes, ancient Grecian settings, and cowboy paraphernalia because, "for whatever reason, censorship laws were enforced more lackadaisically when the subject matter was set in the past" (Auer 2008). Thomas Waugh also notes what he calls the "artistic alibi" as a defence against censorship of naked photographs because "the artistic context [is] one of the few that permits the open circulation of frontal male nudity" (Waugh 1996, 223).

References

Adler, Renata. 1968. "Bleak College Days." *New York Times*, 9 February 1968.

Ahmed, Sara. 2020. "Closing the Door: Complaint as Diversity Work." Public lecture, Kaaitheater, Brussels, Belgium, 18 February 2020.

Anderson, Robert. 1953. *Tea and Sympathy*. New York: Random House.

Armstrong, Elizabeth A., and Suzanna M. Crage. 2006. "Movements and Memory: The Making of the Stonewall Myth." *American Sociological Review* 71, no. 5 (October): 724–51.

Auer, Jeff. 2008. "Cowboys on the Cover of a Magazine." *The Gay & Lesbian Review Worldwide* 15, no. 6 (November-December).

Bordowitz, Gregg. 1993. "The AIDS Crisis Is Ridiculous." In *Queer Looks: Perspectives on Lesbian and Gay Film and Video*, edited by Martha Gever, Pratibha Parmar, and John Greyson, 209–24. New York and London: Routledge.

Brewster, Hugh. 2014. "Outsiders." *The Walrus*, 26 June 2014.

Brice, Lawrence. 1966. "Hart House Is 'Homo House'; Needham." *The Varsity*, 2 December 1966.

Bronski, Michael. 1984. *Culture Clash: The Making of Gay Sensibility*. Boston: South End Press.

Broomer, Stephen. 2016a. *Hamilton Babylon: A History of the McMaster Film Board*. Toronto: University of Toronto Press.

– 2016b. "John Hofsess: Man in Pieces." *Hamilton Arts & Letters* 9, no. 1.

Bruce, Jean, and Gerda Cammaer. 2015. *Forbidden Love: A Queer Film Classic*. Vancouver: Arsenal Pulp Press.

Cagle, R.L. 2019. *Scorpio Rising: A Queer Film Classic*. Vancouver: Arsenal Pulp Press.

Chambers, Stephanie, Jane Farrow, Maureen FitzGerald, et al. 2017. *Any Other Way: How Toronto Got Queer*. Toronto: Coach House Books.

Chauncey, George. 1995. *Gay New York: Gender, Urban Culture, and the Making of the Gay Male World, 1890–1940*. New York: Basic Books.

Churchill, David S. 2004. "Mother Goose's Map: Tabloid Geographies and Gay Male Experience in 1950s Toronto." *Journal of Urban History* 30, no. 6 (September): 826–52.

Cobb, David. 1965. "Movie due in U.K. Monday if Finished Here Sunday." *Toronto Star*, 25 September 1965.

– n.d. "No Canadian Film Industry? Look Again." *Toronto Star*.

Coburn, Teri. 1981. "Jean Lefebvre … On the Fine Art of Festivals." *Cinema Canada* 79 (November): 20–3.

Davidescu, Radu A. 2008. "David Secter's *Winter Kept Us Warm*." Accessed 21 July 2022. http://www.radudavidescu.com/2008/11/david-secters-winter-kept-us-warm-1965.html.

Dean, Heather. 1964. "The Varsity Sport No One Reports." *The Gargoyle/* TWO *Magazine*.

Dean, Tim. 2004. "T.S. Eliot, Famous Clairvoyant." In *Gender, Desire, and Sexuality in T.S. Eliot*, edited by Cassandra Laity and Nancy K. Gish, 43–65. Cambridge: Cambridge University Press.

Dixon, Wheeler Winston. 1997. *The Exploding Eye: A Re-Visionary History of 1960s American Experimental Cinema*. New York: SUNY Press.

Dupuis, Chris. 2013. "Fire Starter: The Images Festival Pays Tribute to Artist David Wojnarowicz." *Xtra Magazine*, 9 April 2013. https://xtramagazine.com/culture/fire-starter-48515.

Dyer, Richard. 1977. *Gays and Film*. London: British Film Institute.

– 2003. *Now You See It: Studies in Lesbian and Gay Film*. 2nd edition. London and New York: Routledge.

Edelman, Lee. 2004. *No Future: Queer Theory and the Death Drive*. Durham, NC, and London: Duke University Press.

Egan, James. 1998. *Challenging the Conspiracy of Silence: My Life as a Canadian Gay Activist*. Toronto: CLGA/Homewood Books.

Eichhorn, Paul. 1997. "Industry by Paul Eichhorn." *Take One* 5, no. 15 (Spring): 52.

Eliot, T.S. 2001. *The Waste Land and Other Writings*. New York: Modern Library.

Farmer, Brett. 2000. *Spectacular Passions: Cinema, Fantasy, Gay Male Spectatorships*. Durham, NC, and London: Duke University Press.

Feldman, Seth. 2006. "Film Education." *The Canadian Encyclopedia*, 7 February 2006. Last edited 16 December 2013. www.thecanadianencyclopedia.ca/en/article/film-education.

Feldman, Seth, and Joyce Nelson. 1977. *Canadian Film Reader*. Toronto: Peter Martin Associates.

Ferry, Antony. 1966. "Top Film Prizes Withheld at Montreal but Toronto Producer Specially Cited." *Toronto Star*, 5 August 1966.

Foucault, Michel. 1978. *The History of Sexuality: Volume 1*. Translated by Robert Hurley. New York: Pantheon Books.

Fraser, Brad. 2021. *All the Rage: A Partial Memoir in Two Acts and a Prologue*. Toronto: Doubleday Canada/Penguin Random House.

Fulford, Robert. 1965. "A Fresh Supply of Mistakes." *Toronto Star*, 19 November 1965.

Getsy, David J. 2017. "Queer Relations." ASAP/*Journal* 2, no. 2 (May): 254–7.

Gever, Martha, Pratibha Parmar, and John Greyson. 1993. *Queer Looks: Perspectives on Lesbian and Gay Film and Video*. New York: Routledge.

Gilmour, Clyde. 1964. "Varsity, Ryerson Students Boldly Making 1 ½-Hour Film." *Toronto Telegram*, n.d.

Ginsberg, Allen. 1959. *Howl and Other Poems*. San Francisco: City Lights Publishers.

Globe and Mail. 1966. "Church Groups Urged to Accept Common-law Partner, Homosexual." 4 June 1966.

Halperin, David M. 2012. *How to Be Gay*. Cambridge, MA, and London: The Belknap Press of Harvard University Press.

Handling, Piers. 2009. "By Way of an Introduction." In *Toronto on Film*, edited by Steve Gravestock and Kate Lawrie Van de Ven, 1–18. Waterloo, ON: Wilfrid Laurier University Press.

Hays, Matthew. 2005a. "Queer Pioneer: David Secter Talks about *Winter Kept Us Warm* 40 Years Later." Accessed 21 July 2022. www.northernstars.ca/secter_david_article.

– 2005b. "A Trailblazing Sleeper of the 60's Is Back." *The Gay & Lesbian Review Worldwide* 12, no. 4 (July/August): 50.

– 2007. "David Secter: Queer Pioneer." In *The View from Here: Conversations with Gay and Lesbian Filmmakers*, edited by Matthew Hays, 290–4. Vancouver: Arsenal Pulp Press.

– 2009. "Where Is Here? Here Is Queer: Four Defining Bent Moments in Toronto Films." In *Toronto on Film*, edited by Steve Gravestock and Kate Lawrie Van de Ven, 137–50. Waterloo, ON: Wilfrid Laurier University Press.

– 2011. "Winter Kept Us Warm." *Cineaste* 36, no. 3 (Summer). Accessed 21 July 2022. https://www.cineaste.com/summer2011/winter-kept-us-warm-web-exclusive.

Helfield, Gillian. 2009. "A Time for Change: The Sixties and Cinéma Direct in Québec." In *The Sixties in Canada: A Turbulent and Creative Decade*, edited by M. Athena Palaeologu, 319–23. Montreal: Black Rose Books.

Herridge, Frances. 1968. "Movie Scene: Fresh Talent from Canada." *New York Post*, 9 February 1968.

Hicklin, Ralph. 1964. "Friendship and $750 Main Ingredients of Campus Film." *Globe and Mail*, 21 November 1964.

Hooper, Tom. 2019. "Queering '69: The Recriminalization of Homosexuality in Canada." *The Canadian Historical Review* 100, no. 2 (June): 257–73.

Horvat, Anamarija. 2021. *Screening Queer Memory: LGBTQ Pasts in Contemporary Film and Television*. London: Bloomsbury Academic.

Jagose, Annamarie. 1996. *Queer Theory: An Introduction*. New York: New York University Press.

Katz, Sidney. 1964a. "The Harsh Facts of Life in the Gay World." *Maclean's*, 27 February 1964.

– 1964b. "The Homosexual Next Door." *Maclean's*, 7 March 1964.

Kinsman, Gary. 1987. *The Regulation of Desire: Sexuality in Canada*. Montreal: Black Rose Books.

– 2013. "Wolfenden in Canada: Within and Beyond Official Discourse in Law Reform Struggles." In *Human Rights, Sexual Orientation and Gender Identity in The Commonwealth: Struggles for Decriminalisation and Change*, edited by Corinne Lennox and Matthew Waites, 183–205. London: School of Advanced Study, University of London.

Kirsch, Max. 2006. "Queer Theory, Late Capitalism, and Internalized Homophobia." *Journal of Homosexuality* 52 (1–2): 19–45.

Knabe, Susan, and Wendy Gay Pearson. 2011. *Zero Patience: A Queer Film Classic*. Vancouver: Arsenal Pulp Press.

Knelman, Martin. 1967. "Movie Underground Surfaces in Toronto." *Toronto Star*, 25 November 1967.

Lim, Dennis. 2010, "It's Actual Life. No, It's Drama. No, It's Both." *New York Times*, 20 August 2010.

Marcorelles, Louis. 1966. "Semaine de la Critique: Winter Kept Us Warm." *Cahiers du cinéma* 179 (June): 47–8.

Martin, Robert K. 1990. "Knights-Errant and Gothic Seducers: The Representation of Male Friendship in Mid-Nineteenth-Century America." In *Hidden from History: Reclaiming the Gay and Lesbian Past*, edited by Martin Bauml Duberman, Martha Vicinus, and George Chauncey Jr, 169–82. New York: Meridian/Penguin.

McLeod, Douglas. 1996. *Lesbian and Gay Liberation in Canada: A Selected Annotated Chronology 1964–1975*. Toronto: ECW Press/Homewood Books.

– 2003. *A Brief History of* GAY, *Canada's First Gay Tabloid, 1964–1966*. Toronto: Homewood Books.

Medjuck, Joe. 1966. "Winter Kept Us Warm." *Take One: The Canadian Film Magazine* 1, no. 1 (September-October): 24.

Melnyk, George. 2004. *One Hundred Years of Canadian Cinema*. Toronto: University of Toronto Press.

Miller, James E. 1977. *T.S. Eliot's Personal Waste Land*. University Park, PA: Penn State University Press.

Morriss, Frank. 1960. "Masterpiece Word to Describe Movie." *Globe and Mail*, 7 April 1960.

– 1964. "NFB Look at Teens Dreary, Ineffectual." *Globe and Mail*, 28 December 1964.

– 1965. "College-Made Film Well Worth Seeing." *Globe and Mail*, 7 December 1965.

– 1966. "Student Movie Goes to Cannes." *Globe and Mail*, 1 March 1966.

Olick, Jeffrey K., and Joyce Robbins. 1998. "Social Memory Studies: From 'Collective Memory' to the Historical Sociology of Mnemonic Practices." *Annual Review of Sociology* 24, 105–40.

Perinot, Claudio. 2011. "Jean Verdenal: An Extraordinary Young Man: T.S. Eliot's mort aux Dardanelles." *South Atlantic Review* 76, no. 3 (Summer), 33–50.

Peter, John. 1952. "A New Interpretation of *The Waste Land*." *Essays in Criticism* 2, no. 3 (July): 242–66.

Pevere, Geoff. 1998. "T.O's an Odd Mecca for Movie Makers." *Toronto Star*, 18 January 1998.

– 2003. "Forgotten Pioneer of the '60s Campus Scene." *Toronto Star*, 31 January 2003.

– 2009. "Flickering City: Toronto on Film until 2002." In *Toronto on Film*,

edited by Steve Gravestock, and Kate Lawrie Van de Ven, 19–68. Toronto: Wilfrid Laurier University Press.
– 2011. "David Secter, the Varsity Visionary." *Toronto Star*, 24 June 2011.
Porter, McKenzie. 1965. "McKenzie Porter … Tells about the Movie Describing Life on a Toronto Campus Winter Keeps [*sic*] Us Warm." *Toronto Telegram*, 15 January 1965.
Pratley, Gerald. 1965. "Review of Winter Kept Us Warm." *Toronto Telegram*, n.d.
Purdon, Noel. 1976. "Gay Cinema." *Cinema Papers* 10 (September-October): 115–19, 179.
Rich, B. Ruby. 2013. *New Queer Cinema: The Director's Cut*. Durham, NC, and London: Duke University Press.
Rigney, Ann. 2016. "Cultural Memory Studies: Mediation, Narrative, and the Aesthetic." In *Routledge International Handbook of Memory Studies*, 65–76. London: Routledge.
Robertson, Heather. 1966. "Winter Kept Us Warm: A Very Hot Movie." *Winnipeg Tribune*, 8 January 1966.
Rohrs, Lauren. 2019. "The Homosexual Male Gaze: Normalizing Homosexuality through the Use of Heteronormative Narrative Techniques in Film." CINEJ *Cinema Journal* 7, no. 2 (Spring/Summer): 6–22.
Roud, Richard. 1966a. "Festival 66: Cannes." *Sight and Sound* 35, no. 3 (Summer): 125–7, 154.
– 1966b. "Richard Roud Reporting from the Cannes Film Festival." *The Guardian*, 23 May 1966.
Russell, Glenda M., and Janis S. Bohan. 2005. "The Gay Generation Gap: Communicating across the LGBT Generational Divide." *The Policy Journal of The Institute of Gay and Lesbian Strategic Studies* 8, no. 1 (December): 1–8.
Secter, David. 1964. "Will 'the Great Canadian Film' Be Shot at U of T?" *The Varsity*, 30 October 1964.
– 1965. "Lack of Experience Helps: How to Make a Do-It-Yourself Movie without Money." *Globe and Mail*, 17 November 1965.

Sedgwick, Eve Kosofsky. 1993. *Tendencies*, London: Routledge.

Seymour-Jones, Carole. 2001. *The Painted Shadow: The Life of Vivienne Eliot, First Wife of T.S. Eliot*. New York: Anchor Books/Random House.

Sismondo, Christine. 2017. "Headline Homophobia Tops Tabloid Treatments!" In *Any Other Way: How Toronto Got Queer*, edited by Stephanie Chambers, Jane Farrow, Maureen FitzGerald, et al., 246–9. Toronto: Coach House Books.

Stinnett, Graham. 2019. "Meeting Places." *Manitoba Gay and Lesbian Archives*. Accessed 24 October 2020. https://umanitoba.ca/libraries/units/archives/digital/ gay_lesbian/places.html.

Stoller, James. 1967a. "16 mm (Review of *Bike Boy*)." *The Village Voice*, 19 October 1967.

– 1967b. "16 mm (Review of *Portrait of Jason*)." *The Village Voice*, 5 October 1967.

– 1968. "16 mm (Review of *Winter Kept Us Warm*)." *The Village Voice*, 15 February 1968.

Thomas, June. 2011. "The Gay Bar: Is It Dying?" *Slate*, 27 June 2011. www.slate.com/id/2297604.

Thomas, Kevin. 1968. "'Winter' on Screen at Cinematheques." *Los Angeles Times*, 16 May 1968.

Toronto Star. 1963. "Church Fails the Homosexual." 15 June 1963.

– 1964. "Homosexuality Sin, Not Crime – Church Panel." 10 March 1964.

Vaillancourt, Julie. 2023. *À tout prendre* et *Il était une fois dans l'Est*. Montreal and Kingston: McGill-Queen's University Press.

Variety. 1966. "Winter Kept Us Warm."

The Varsity. 1969. "Edward as Marlowe Would Have Played Him." 17 January 1969.

Waugh, Thomas. 1982. "Uncovering a Forgotten Canadian Gay Film – from 1965." *The Body Politic*, no. 83 (May): 36.

– 1996. *Hard to Imagine: Gay Male Eroticism in Photography and Film from Their Beginnings to Stonewall*. New York: Columbia University Press.

– 1999. "Cinemas, Nations, Masculinities: The Martin Walsh Memorial Lecture." *Canadian Journal of Film Studies* 8, no. 1 (Spring): 8–44.
– 2001. "Fairy Tales of Two Cities, Or Queer Nation(s)/Urban Cinema(s)." *Canadian Journal of Film Studies* 10, no. 2 (Fall): 102–25.
– 2006. *The Romance of Transgression in Canada: Queering Sexualities, Nations, Cinemas*. Montreal and Kingston: McGill-Queens University Press.
Wells, Jonathan. 2015. "How the Internet Revolutionised LGBT Life." *The Telegraph*, 12 November 2015.
Weston, Kath. 1997. *Families We Choose: Lesbians, Gays, Kinship*. New York: Columbia University Press.
Wilczak, Kate. 2002. "Nostalgia Is Gay: 6T5 Alum's Film Handles Homosexuality with Charm." *The Independent*, 28 February 2002.
Winnipeg Free Press. 1965. "Two Years ahead of Orson."
Youngblood, Gene. 1968. "Underground Cinema." *Los Angeles Free Press*, 24 May 1968.
Zeldin, Arthur. 1964. "Winter Kept Us Warm." *The Varsity*, 20 November 1964.
– 1965a. "Arthur Zeldin Writes About … Another U of T Movie Club." *The Varsity*, 29 January 1965.
– 1965b. "Notes as Winter Ends." *The Varsity*, 19 March 1965.
– 1965c. "Take Note," *The Varsity*, 22 January 1965.
– 1965d. "Winter Movie." *The Varsity*, 10 December 1965.

Personal Interviews

Janet Amos. 20 November 2020.
Bruce Bell. 15 April 2020.
James Dubro. 16 November 2020.
Joy Fielding. 16 November 2020.
Robert Fothergill. 2 November 2020.
Matthew Hays. 9 December 2020.

Paul Hoffert. 19 November 2020.
Andrew Kushner. 28 May 2020.
Joe Medjuck. 30 November 2020.
David Secter. 17 December 2019, 30 November 2020, 7 December 2020, 14 December 2020, 30 December 2020, 30 March 2021, 10 May 2021, 26 May 2021, and 23 December 2021.
Joel Secter. 13 November 2020.
Ron B. Thomson. 7 December 2020.
Thomas Waugh. 11 December 2020.

Filmography

À tout prendre (Take It All). Claude Jutra. Canada. 1963. 100 minutes.
"After All, Who's Art Morrison?" *Wojeck*. Ronald Weyman. Canada. 1967. 50 minutes.
And No Birds Sing. Victor Cowie. Canada. 1969. 42 minutes.
The Best of Secter & the Rest of Secter. Joel Secter. Canada. 2005. 58 minutes.
Bike Boy. Andy Warhol. USA. 1967. 96 minutes.
The Bitter Ash. Larry Kent. Canada. 1963. 80 minutes.
Black Christmas. Bob Clark. Canada. 1974. 98 minutes.
The Children's Hour. William Wyler. USA. 1961. 107 minutes.
Crimes of the Future. David Cronenberg. Canada. 1970. 63 minutes.
Délivrez-nous du mal (Deliver Us from Evil). Jean-Claude Lord. Canada. 1969. 82 minutes.
"Every Tenth Man: A Study of Homosexuality." *Other Voices*. Jim Guthro. Canada. 24 November 1964. 30 minutes.
Flaming Creatures. Jack Smith. USA. 1963. 42 minutes.
Fortune and Men's Eyes. Harvey Hart. Canada/USA. 1971. 102 minutes.
The Fox. Mark Rydell. Canada. 1967. 110 minutes.

From the Drain. David Cronenberg. Canada. 1967. 14 minutes.
Goin' Down the Road. Don Shebib. Canada. 1970. 90 minutes.
The Handmaid's Tale. TV series. Bruce Miller. USA. 2017.
Il était une fois dans l'Est (Once Upon a Time in the East). André Brassard and Michel Tremblay. Canada. 1974. 100 minutes.
The Leather Boys. Sidney J. Furie. United Kingdom. 1964. 108 minutes.
Leaving Metropolis. Brad Fraser. Canada. 2002. 89 minutes.
Lilies. John Greyson. Canada. 1996. 95 minutes.
Love with the Proper Guppy. David Secter. Canada. 1964. 8 minutes.
Nobody Waved Good-bye. Don Owen. Canada. 1964. 80 minutes.
Outrageous! Richard Benner. Canada. 1977. 100 minutes.
Pleasure Faire. Terry Nowak. Canada/USA. 1963–64. 15 minutes.
Portrait of Jason. Shirley Clarke. USA. 1967. 105 minutes.
Pour la suite du monde. Michel Brault, Marcel Carrière, and Pierre Perrault. Canada. 1963. 105 minutes.
Les Quatre Cents Coups (The 400 Blows). François Truffaut. France. 1959. 99 minutes.
Rebel Without a Cause. Nicholas Ray. USA. 1955. 111 minutes.
Red River. Howard Hawks. USA. 1948. 127 minutes.
Sebastiane. Derek Jarman. United Kingdom. 1976. 85 minutes.
The Servant. Joseph Losey. United Kingdom. 1963. 116 minutes.
Scorpio Rising. Kenneth Anger. USA. 1963. 28 minutes.
Seul ou avec d'autres (Alone or with Others). Denys Arcand, Denis Héroux, and Stéphane Venne. Canada. 1962. 64 minutes.
Stereo. David Cronenberg. Canada. 1969. 65 minutes.
Tangerine. Sean Baker. USA. 2015. 98 minutes.
Tarnation. Jonathan Caouette. USA. 2003. 91 minutes.
Tea and Sympathy. Vincente Minnelli. USA. 1956. 122 minutes.
Transfer. David Cronenberg. Canada. 1966. 7 minutes.
Victim. Basil Dearden. United Kingdom. 1961 96 minutes.

United in Anger: A History of ACT UP. Jim Hubbard. USA. 2012. 90 minutes.
Wings. William Wellman. USA. 1927. 111 minutes.
Winter Kept Us Warm. David Secter. Canada. 1965. 81 minutes.
Zero Patience. John Greyson. Canada. 1993. 95 minutes.

Index

Page numbers in italics indicate a figure.